ASK
YOUR
FATHER

Conversations with Pop about
War, Food, and Following Your Dreams

TONY & LORRAINE WASOWICZ

Published by Whippet Tales

Photographs from the authors' collection and courtesy of B-26.com and Guidance Aviation.

Title: Ask Your Father:

Conversations with Pop about War, Food, and Following Your Dreams /

Tony and Lorraine Wasowicz

Printed in the United States of America

ISBN 979-8-218-14375-6

FOR POP'S CREW

Contents

ASK YOUR FATHER

Prologue

The Focke-Wulf-190 German fighter plane burst out of the high clouds of the Belgian sky and made straight for the Allied B-26 bomber EXTERMINATOR. A flurry of shells erupted out of the fighter's 20mm nose cannon and peppered the bomber, hitting the right engine and exploding inside the cramped cockpit and navigation compartment. In an instant, fire engulfed the interior of the B-26, and thick smoke blinded the crew. The pilot, twenty-one-year-old Flight Officer Barney Wasowicz, on his 18th mission over enemy-occupied France, struggled with the controls as all hydraulic links were severed. It was obvious the aircraft was going down. What was not clear was if any of the six crew members would make it out alive.

I stood staring at the little boy peeing into the basin. He was dwarfed by his large, ornate dwelling place, the niche on the *Rue du Chêne*. Was it really him? I thought, surprised and frankly disappointed. He appeared to be about the size of a six-month-old child, and he was wearing a jaunty red and blue soccer outfit, complete with tall sport socks. Surely the symbol of all things Belgian must be more than two feet tall, I thought. We had come across the statue quite by accident. Earlier that day, my wife Lorraine and I had arrived in Brussels, the last city of our European vacation, the last city of my father's European tour of duty in World War II. Although the *Manneken Pis* was first on my long list of things to see, we went to lunch, leaving the guidebook at the hotel. The afternoon was cold and damp, and after lunch, we were walking the magnificent *Grote Markt*, when suddenly, we happened upon a corner where a crowd was gathered. I'm sure I would have walked right past if not for the excited mass of selfie-wielding tourists clambering for a glimpse of something. At six feet three inches, I had the advantage, looking over their heads. There it was, the iconic *Manneken Pis*. I stopped Lo and pointed it out to her.

"But it's tiny!" she protested, craning her neck to see above the heads of the crowd. "And why is it wearing that outfit?"

"I guess he's a soccer fan," I laughed. But as we moved about trying to get a better look, I found myself growing annoyed. Maybe it was the pushy jumble of tourists, grinning and laughing and waving cell phones on sticks as they jostled for a photo with the famous bronze boy. Maybe I was just tired. But shouldn't a 400-year-old bronze statue that had survived World War II be shown a little respect? Instead, the little guy was dressed up like a doll. It seemed undignified.

"I don't get it," Lo said.

"Me neither," I replied. "Maybe this is what Rick Steves meant when he said that Brussels is a great city with a cheesy mascot."

My father had seen the statue decades ago, after the war, and he told me that it was small, but this was ridiculous. Nevertheless, the important thing was to get a picture, so I handed Lo the camera, and she snapped a few shots of me with the bronze imp.

Why did I find all this hilarity so irritating?

Manneken Pis has a long, fascinating history, a history that I learned about only after I'd seen it. Designed by Jérôme Duquesnoy the Elder in 1619, this 24-inch bronze statue of a "Little Pissing Man" replicates an earlier statue, long gone, of a small man urinating into the fountain's basin. At that time, and for many years after, the little man was naked, except on special occasions. These days, however, if you want to see him naked, you must go to the Brussels City Museum, where Duquesnoy's 1619 bronze statue is kept under glass. The statue we were looking at was yet another replica cast in 1965 after Duquesnoy's sculpture was kidnapped, broken, and flung into the Brussels-Charleroi Canal. After it was rescued, the battered statue was restored and stowed safely in the Museum.

Standing there on the corner, I noted that few of the tourists were looking at the statue itself. Still gazing into their phones, each viewer eventually wandered away toward the gleaming windows of the surrounding giftshops, all displaying row upon row of *Manneken Pis* souvenirs, from bottle openers to lamps to full scale chocolate replicas. The stuff was selling like hotcakes. Or, since we were in Belgium, like waffles.

"You want a *Manneken* corkscrew?" Lo offered. "Or a keychain? I'm buying."

"Awful tempting," I said. "This is all so trippy. Can you imagine what it was like in 1945, when Pop was standing here?"

Seventy-three years earlier, after being liberated from a German prison camp, my father had found himself standing where I now stood. When he told me about it, while I was planning this trip, I had pictured rather a different scene, a quiet setting for a moment of solemn reflection. Now that I was here, among the merry vacationers, I could only shake my head, a little put off by the mirth of the spectacle: a venerable bronze statue wearing doll clothes, surrounded by a buzzing swarm of humanity, posing, arms extended, grinning at themselves.

I stepped back from the crowd and the shops. Closing my eyes, I imagined the roar of warbirds flying low overhead against the gray sky. Unlike its industrial neighbor, Rotterdam, which had been leveled by the Nazis, the landmarks of Brussels had escaped significant damage. When I opened my eyes, the buildings retained their ancient splendor. Maybe, I thought, the problem is *me*. Lighten up, I told myself. He is *peeing* after all. And everyone else seemed thoroughly pleased with the sharp-dressed little man.

I later learned that the tradition of dressing *Manneken Pis* in costumes dates to 1615. But the custom gained steam in the 20th Century and is now elevated to a ceremony advertised and carried out several times a week. For decades now, *Manneken Pis* has been decked out in bespoke outfits, a new one every few days or so, sent from around the world. There's even a museum displaying an archive of around 1,000 outfits he's donned. Since the early 20th Century, he's been dressed in most everything you can think of: Dracula's cape, a beekeeper's bonnet, Mozart's brocade, and even a United States Air Force uniform.

More importantly, I learned that *Manneken Pis* is meant to symbolize the people of Brussels, who are known for their ironic sense of humor—*zwanze*—and their independence of mind. Apparently, my father had been quite taken with the monument. It had been an odd highlight of his brief time in Brussels. I stepped further back from the crowd and the fountain; I tried to erase the carnival atmosphere—the giftshops, the soccer costume, the selfie-sticks—and transport myself to the summer of 1945:

One night, on a lark, my father and a friend drive a jeep around Brussels, with two hundred dollars and a bottle of gin. They're celebrating the end of the war. Sometime around dawn, they turn the corner of the *Rue du Chêne*, and there in front of them is the *Manneken Pis*. Gone is the black swastika of the Third Reich which had recently been torn down. Behind *Manneken Pis* are Great Britain's Union Jack, America's Stars and Stripes, France's Tricolore, and Russia's Hammer and Sickle. The air is cool and there is a sound of water. The two soldiers hop out of their jeep and approach the fountain, following the arc of the stream up to the bronze boy, serenely peeing in the rosy morning light. For a moment the soldiers pause, puzzled. They look at each other. And then, suddenly, peals of laughter ring out, echoing in the quiet street. They laugh so hard, they almost fall down. They clap each other on the shoulders and point up at the flowing stream. Still laughing, they shake their heads, climb back into the jeep, and head to the airbase to hitch a ride back to France.

Seeing the *Manneken Pis* was the only detail that my father recalled about his night on the town, so it must have struck a chord. I could see how Pop, with his rebellious individualism and his ironic humor, must have identified with this absurd symbol of Brussels. Little by little, I was beginning to understand how the world appeared to my father all those years ago.

I wished I could have been there.

Maybe that was it. I was envious. Not just because my father and his buddy were in Europe in the old days. But because they had come here on a mission to save the world. I had wanted this trip to be something more than the typical European vacation. I meant it to be a kind of pilgrimage. Lo and I had admired the art and architecture; we had reveled in the cuisine and culture. But every tour of an ancient church and every lunch of mussels and white asparagus was accompanied by a sense of gratitude. In their quest to take over the world, the Nazis had destroyed much of Europe. My father helped to stop them.

CHAPTER 1

Low Expectations

Once you have tasted flight, you will forever walk the earth with your eyes turned skyward, for there you have been, and there you will always long to return.

—Leonardo da Vinci

After climbing over 2,500 feet on the steep, winding interstate through the saguaro stippled Arizona desert, I pulled the rental car into the McDonald's parking lot, just as I had done countless other times. The day before, I had flown in from California to visit my parents, and it was not going well. We were all on edge, not enjoying ourselves with our usual good-humored banter. And no wonder. This was my first visit since I had been here for my oldest brother's memorial service. It was still a shock to my whole family to think that, after a short, intense battle with cancer, Bill was gone. He had passed away in December, and Lo and I had driven down to attend the service and stay for Christmas. Now, only a few months later, my mother and father were trying to figure out how to deal with the fact that their first-born son had preceded them in death.

I had another thirty minutes of driving until we hit my other brother's home outside of Prescott, and the fast-food giant was our usual, reliable pit stop. With little of interest to talk about, I had been driving on autopilot, barely noticing the spectacular array of venerable cactus beneath the vast Arizona sky. I parked the car, and my mom made a beeline for the restroom while I helped my father out of the back seat. Knowing the answer already, I asked anyway.

"Hey Pop, you want a little something to eat while we're here?"

"No," he replied, without hesitation. I tried to reason with him.

"But Jeff said we wouldn't be having dinner until around six. You really should have something to eat before then. Maybe just some fries, at least?"

"No!" he snapped back. "I haven't eaten fast food since I came back from the war. I'm not about to start now."

I couldn't argue with that, so I gave up and led him to the restroom. On the way in, we passed Mom, hungrily unwrapping a Filet-O-Fish sandwich. She would never take a pass on food, fast or otherwise.

Before we got back on the road, I called Jeff to give him our ETA. Jeff and I were more than brothers, we were best friends, and talking to him was a relief. Besides, we had a lot of catching up to do. We kept it brief, going over the plan for our weekend. We would soon have plenty of time to visit, or so I thought. After I hung up, I broke the news to Mom and Pop.

"Um, yeah.... So, Jeff said he's going to barbecue some ribs." I paused. "And he's inviting a few friends over."

Simultaneous groans from my parents.

"Why does he do this every time we come?" Pop grumbled. "I don't want a party. I don't want to see anybody. I can't see anybody anyway." Practically blinded by macular degeneration, my father felt most comfortable with familiar people and settings.

"Shouldn't be a big deal," I said casually, trying to reassure them. "I don't think it's exactly a party. Just a few friends over for some grilled ribs and dessert."

"We'd rather it was just family," Mom insisted.

"It *is* family, mostly," I lied. Personally, I shared their disappointment and exasperation. I had also been looking forward to some quality face time with my brother. But I wasn't surprised. Jeff had always been an incurable extrovert, determined to win friends and influence people wherever he went. He and his wife had a large home where they loved to bring people together and entertain. I tried to smooth it over.

"It'll just be Jeff and Dawn and us. The girls will be there," I added. "I think Brooke has some friends staying. And then it'll just be Peter and Carolyn—you know them. And maybe a couple of other guys Jeff said he just met. He said they're really nice."

It was a losing argument. It was going to be a party all right.

Never underestimate the law of low expectations. Mom was soon visiting warmly with her granddaughters and their friends. Meanwhile, Pop and I found ourselves deep in conversation with one of Jeff's new friends, an airplane enthusiast named John Stonecipher. He had a quick, winning smile and the sparkling, adventuresome eyes of an Indiana Jones. It was impossible not to love the guy at first sight. For most of the evening, John had been entertaining us with his encyclopedic knowledge of all things aviation, especially warbirds. To my surprise, Pop began to talk about *his* World War II warbird, commenting that the airplane he flew, the Martin B-26 Marauder, was virtually extinct, and lamenting that the few that had survived the scrap heap weren't flight-worthy. He hadn't mentioned the B-26 to me in years.

A B-26 MARTIN MARAUDER BOMBING A BRIDGE

The Martin B-26 Marauder was arguably the most bad-ass airplane deployed in WWII. Its birth came about because of an Army Air Corps request set forth in January 1939 for a twin-engine, high-speed, medium-altitude bomber. The Glenn L. Martin Company quickly submitted a design that had been drafted by Peyton Magruder, who was only 27 years old.

This kid was well ahead of his time when he designed this drag racer of a bomber. She was devastatingly fast and equally dangerous to fly. Despite early problems and heated controversy, the aircraft eventually proved so successful that a total of 5,288 were produced between February 1941 and March 1945. The 9th Air Force rated it the most accurate bomber available in the final months of the war in Europe and, in the end, the B-26 had the lowest combat loss rate of any U.S. aircraft used during the war.

"Actually, there *is* one B-26 left, sir," John said. "At least, one left in flying condition, anyway. It's in a private museum called Fantasy of Flight in Florida."

"Oh, yeah?" Pop's eyes suddenly lit up.

"Oh, yeah!" John grinned.

I could only imagine what the B-26 meant to my father. I supposed it was like a best friend, a trusty horse, or a beloved dog that you never expected to see again. Out of the blue, Pop found a kindred spirit in John.

To say that John was obsessed with aircraft is an understatement. In 1998, he single-handedly founded the Guidance Aviation helicopter school at the Prescott Airport, starting with one helicopter and a single pilot. In just fifteen years, the school had evolved into a leading collegiate helicopter flight training academy, with a fleet of twenty-six aircraft, over one hundred employees, and hundreds of graduates working throughout the aviation industry. In his spare time, John was renovating a battered Alaska bush plane. Jeff was in the business of land development and had recently met John during talks of expanding the helicopter school.

My father stared at John, absorbing the astonishing news, shaking his head, and smiling. The news of an intact B-26 was nothing, however, compared to what John said next.

"I have an idea, sir," he ventured with a little smile. "My company just bought a new airplane, a real nice one. If you're interested, I'd like to fly you and your family to Florida to reunite you with your aircraft."

At first, I wasn't sure Pop had heard him correctly. I wasn't sure I had either.

"Wow," was all Pop could manage to reply after a long pause. My father, the veteran combat pilot, was known for his even demeanor and steady nerves, but this thrilling proposal left him completely speechless.

"It's totally up to you, sir," John continued. "We can go whenever you'd like. Maybe in a few months so you can get organized. It'll give you a chance to put together your crew."

"My *crew*, eh?" This was an offer Pop could not refuse. Despite his poor vision and difficulty getting around, there was no way my father could pass up the opportunity to see his beloved airplane again after bailing out of her seventy years ago. And, at ninety-two years old, he would have no other opportunities like this.

"I'm in!" I interjected. This was a once-in-a-lifetime opportunity for me as well, and there was no way I was going to miss out. Like my father, as a kid, I was always thinking about airplanes—my very first crayon drawings in kindergarten were of birds and airplanes. And I had dreamed, early on, of going to the Air Force Academy and flying jets. But unlike my father, I didn't have the required perfect vision, so flying jets remained a dream. To this day, I spend my waiting time at airports, staring out the window, mesmerized by jumbo jets taking off and landing.

"I'm sure Jeff will want to go, too," I added. "Wait till he hears this! What do you think, Pop?"

"Wow," he said again.

"Then it's set, sir!" John beamed. "We're going to Fantasy of Flight! This is gonna be great. I personally know the man who owns the museum, name's Kermit Weeks. It's not open to the public, but I know he'll give you the red carpet. And he's a pilot, too. He was able to get the airplane into flying condition and flew it to the MacDill airshow and back a few years ago. Might've been the last flight ever for a B-26."

In a matter of minutes, it was settled. We were going on a mission to Florida to see the very last flight-worthy Martin B-26 Marauder.

Later, just as Jeff's wife, Dawn, was announcing it was time for dessert, John made yet another sweet offer.

"And if you guys aren't doing anything tomorrow morning, I'd love to give you a tour of my helicopter school and show you the airplane we'll be flying to Florida. She's brand new—a real beauty."

It seemed the magic of low expectations had turned a difficult visit with my parents into the prospect of an incredible adventure.

Early the next morning the adventure began. We chatted excitedly over coffee, accompanied by some of Dawn's fresh baked cinnamon rolls.

"The B-26 had such a bad reputation because it was a difficult airplane to learn to fly," Pop was saying. "It was the only airplane that went directly from the drawing board to the production line."

"How come?" I asked.

"We were at war. Planes were badly needed. So the usual steps for acceptance by the Army were ignored."

"Oh, so that's why they called it the *widow-maker*!" I said.

Pop laughed. "Yes, but once you did learn to fly it, it was a wonderful airplane." He was looking up at the ceiling, the B-26 in his mind's eye.

"Man, that must have been amazing, flying one of those things," I said.

"Scary, too!" he said. "But before my first in-flight lesson, I had to attend ground school and learn everything about the plane."

He was about to go on, when Mom suddenly interjected, "What are you guys doing for lunch? Do you want to take some snacks along for later?"

"Nah," I told her. "We shouldn't be gone that long. We'll probably get a quick tour of the school, take a peek at the plane, and be done. John's a busy guy, after all."

"*Chodzmy, tutti!*" Pop barked, getting up from the table. This was Polish for *Let's go, everyone!*

Brows furrowed, Mom studied my father as he put on his jacket to go.

"Barney, did you put on your sunscreen? It's going to be hot today so you should take your cap along as well. And make sure you take that bottle of water. I put it in the refrigerator to keep it cold." She hovered around him, smoothing out the wrinkles in his jacket.

Pop muttered something under his breath as Mom carefully adjusted a cap on his head and then retrieved the water from the fridge.

"And make sure you take your cane," she continued. "You'll probably be doing some walking, and I don't want you getting too tired."

"Stop pestering me," he retorted. "I can take care of myself. I'll be fine."

"And you need to make sure..." she continued, insistently.

"I'll be fine," he snapped back and shuffled out the door as Mom, not so sure, followed us to the car.

"Have fun!" she called as we pulled away, waving.

TONY, POP, AND JEFF WITH THE PILATUS PC-12

John was right—his new airplane was beautiful: a brand-new Swiss-built Pilatus PC-12, considered to be one of the finest single-engine aircraft in the world. Jeff and I circled the plane in the hangar with Pop, admiring and praising her lines.

John broke the spell, announcing, "Okay, guys, let's get right to it. I have a certified pilot for her on-site and he's ready to go if you'd like to take a quick spin."

Our jaws dropped in unison.

Before we could respond, he strode to the back of the hangar and began dragging over a hydraulic aircraft tug. Within minutes the pilot walked through the door. While Pop stood gaping in disbelief, the rest of us helped push the airplane out of the hanger. Then, just like that, we all boarded the plane and soared into the Arizona sky. While Jeff and I sat in the cushy back seats of the Pilatus with John, discussing details for the upcoming trip to Florida, Pop was perched in the co-pilot's seat, beaming. We all wore headsets so we could hear the chatter between the pilot and Pop, along with the airport control tower.

The pilot took us on a sky tour of the spectacular desert plains and mountains surrounding Prescott and Dewey. After he had banked the aircraft back toward the airport, we heard him say, "Barney—sir—would you like to take over the controls for a bit?"

"I'd love to!" Pop said without hesitation.

Along with the rest of the crew in the back of the Pilatus, I sat stunned as Pop immediately executed a series of sweeping bank turns, all smooth as a whistle. The pilot turned in his seat to look back at us, a boyish grin on his face.

"He's on the ball! He's right on the ball!" he yelled back at us. I recognized the reference. In older aircraft, coordinated flight—up and down and side to side—is indicated by keeping a BB-sized ball centered in an instrument called the inclinometer. When you're on the ball, your turns are perfect. My ninety-two-year-old, mostly blind father, behind the controls of an aircraft he knew nothing about, was carving perfect turns in the sky.

It didn't take long before the thrill of seeing my father piloting the snazzy Pilatus wore off, and the anxiety of seeing him settle in for a long cross-country flight set in. Midway through my flight back home to northern California, I was gazing out the window at the flat, monotonous desert plains east of the Sierras when I noticed an ache in my lower back. Nothing serious, just the usual kind of annoying cramp from sitting too long in a confined Economy seat. I had been in the air for just over an hour—only another hour to go. I could get up to stretch my legs and walk around since I was traveling in a commercial jumbo jet with relatively spacious aisles and restrooms. I could distract myself with the book I had brought along, or watch a movie.

But the little pain in my back triggered a cascade of ominous thoughts. Here I was, middle-aged and fit, yet feeling uncomfortable after only an hour. I visualized my father, a very old man, sitting on a much smaller airplane for most of a day. A quick spin in the Pilatus was one thing, but a trip to the Florida panhandle? His longest journey in years was our periodic two-hour car trip to Prescott, rest stop at the Golden Arches included.

I mentally catalogued my concerns about Pop. First, the injuries he had sustained while bailing out of his B-26 had left him with severe arthritis in his neck and back. Chronic pain was a way of life; any prolonged inactivity made it worse. At night he slept in an overstuffed recliner chair, getting up every few hours to make coffee and pace the floor. Second, he had irritable bowel syndrome, necessitating frequent trips to the bathroom. The Pilatus, of course, had a toilet, but it was tucked into a cramped closet. Third, he had advanced macular degeneration and could barely make out objects, fuzzy and shadowy, directly in front of him. He certainly couldn't see anything out the window or read a book. Fourth, his hearing aids were high maintenance, their efficiency compromised by background noise and the size and acoustics of the space he was in. He was always fidgeting with them, taking them out, adjusting them, and fumbling with his stash of tiny batteries when they gave out. Fifth, he was subject to persistent, paralyzing headaches....

"Getting old isn't for sissies!" I remember my father saying.

I writhed around in my seat, sipping from my plastic cup of ginger ale, and eventually the ache went away. But the anxiety remained. If just living everyday life at home was a major challenge for Pop, how in the world, I wondered, could he manage a cross-country expedition to Florida? Suddenly the Fantasy of Flight trip that John had generously proposed seemed indeed just a fantasy. Maybe in all the excitement we had ignored common sense and reason. Perhaps it was simply too late for Pop.

My fears, I quickly realized, were mine alone to bear. I didn't dare share my concerns because I already knew the response I would get.

"I'll be fine," Pop would say, the same declaration I'd heard countless times in response to my mother's futile arguments. And if he wouldn't listen to his wife, his life-long co-pilot, he certainly wouldn't listen to his youngest son.

I looked out the window. The airliner's flight path took us directly over Yosemite National Park, and as the flat plains gave way to sinuous mountain peaks and valleys, I spied the unmistakable glowing top of Half Dome, 35,000 feet below. Somehow, the awesome sight of the shining granite rock formation reassured me. I knew I had to accept that I had no control. There was really no choice in the matter. The mission must be carried out, and I would be there, not to worry, but to help make it happen.

"Onward and upward," Pop would declare every time he hit one of life's speedbumps. I thought about another of my father's favorite, oft recited lines:

"I'll rest when I'm dead."

And so will I, I thought with a smile.

CHAPTER 2

Fantasy of Flight

Only six B-26s still exist, and this is the only one capable of flight. Because of its small wing area, the B-26 was nicknamed the "Widow-Maker." MacDill Air Force Base in Tampa was the main training base for B-26 crews during the War. As a result of a short series of training accidents after take-off, the undeserved phrase "One a Day in Tampa Bay" came about. In 1998, I flew this aircraft into MacDill for their annual airshow and back to Fantasy of Flight without incident. This was the last B-26 to ever leave a MacDill runway, so hopefully the curse has been broken.

—Kermit Weeks Founder, Fantasy of Flight Air Museum

Onward and upward. Without further trepidation, I returned to Arizona a few months later, and again drove my father to Prescott, where we met Jeff and John at the airport. The same pilot, Jason, who took us on the joy ride, was standing alongside the Pilatus PC-12, waving to us as we piled out of the car. Three others were talking in the shade of the hangar. Along for the ride were Steve, my brother-in-law; Dave, an associate with the school; and Bryan Matuskey, yet another friend of Jeff's. This event was going to be a highlight of a lifetime, and John was making sure to seize the moment. Bryan, a professional videographer with the helicopter school, was going to document Pop's reunion with his warbird. Everyone was talking at once, nervous and excited to board the Pilatus again, this time bound for the Fantasy of Flight Air Museum in Polk City, Florida. When the last of our gear had been loaded into the cargo compartment, John disappeared back into the hangar. He emerged a minute later, carrying a large cardboard box.

John set the box on the tarmac and called to us. "Hey, guys, before you get on board, check this out!" He tore open the box and pulled out a pile of brand-new custom Guidance Aviation flight jackets, one for each of us. "Put these on," he ordered. We obeyed and then lined up in front of the aircraft, laughing. "Now it's official—we're a crew!" he said. Proud and purposeful in our new uniforms, we boarded the PC-12, bound for Polk City.

After takeoff, once everyone settled in, I took out the papers in the folder I had brought along. Anticipating that the flight to Florida would be a long one, I had come prepared with several pages of internet research. I intended to pass the time reading it to my father, but throughout the long flight, he sat contentedly in the co-pilot's seat, so I had only myself to entertain. At Jeff's house, months before, John had talked about the museum and its owner, but until now, I had virtually no idea who this mysterious man was or any details about his collection. A little research had revealed a remarkable character.

Kermit Weeks's passion for aviation began quite early. As a teenager, he not only learned to fly, but he also began constructing his first home-built airplane. At the age of twenty, he was competing in aerobatic flying competitions while pursuing an aeronautical engineering degree. With an eye toward improving the flight dynamics of competition aircraft, he designed and constructed the "Weeks Special" and qualified for the United States Aerobatics Team. Executed in airplanes and gliders, for training, recreation, entertainment, and sport, aerobatics is the performance of extreme flying maneuvers, sometimes called "stunt flying." In fact, some of these maneuvers were used during World War II aerial combat, or dogfights, between fighter aircraft. Mastery of these daring twists and turns and loops and rolls gave fighter pilots a tactical advantage. Today, aerobatic flying competitions are an international phenomenon, the Olympic Games of the skies.

In 1978, at the World Aerobatics Championships held in Czechoslovakia, Weeks was runner-up among sixty-one competitors worldwide. Subsequently, Weeks placed in the top three in the world five times, winning a total of twenty medals in World Aerobatics Championship competitions. Weeks would go on to be inducted into the Experimental Aircraft Association Hall of Fame in 2005 and recognized as a "Living Legend of Aviation" in 2006.

Not content with achieving mere flying expertise, Weeks's passion for aviation eventually expanded into the restoration and preservation of vintage aircraft. In 1978, he founded the non-profit Weeks Air Museum in Miami, and as his collection of vintage aircraft grew, he realized he needed more room—a lot more room. By 1992, he had completed development plans for a 300-acre site near Polk City, Florida. Thus began his dream of Fantasy of Flight. It began inauspiciously, as that same year Hurricane Andrew struck the Miami area, virtually destroying the entire facility and damaging most of the vintage aircraft within it. Undaunted, Weeks slowly began repairing and restoring the damaged airplanes; just three years later, Fantasy of Flight opened its doors. Today, Kermit's collection includes around 120 vintage aircraft, although not all are on display at any given time.

Amazingly, there is more—the talents of Kermit Weeks, I learned, were not limited to flying, constructing, collecting, and renovating airplanes. He has also written two books for children, created an audio CD of stories inspired by his vintage aircraft collection, and produced a behind-the-scenes documentary on Fantasy of Flight featured on PBS.

At lunchtime, we made a quick pitstop at a small Texas airport for refueling and lunch, but soon, we were back in the air. Pop was heading to the co-pilot's seat when Dave said he had something for him. It was a big envelope full of letters, handwritten by local schoolchildren. Dave's wife Francoise was their teacher, and it had been her idea to have the kids write notes to our dad, the war hero. Jeff and I took turns describing the cute crayon drawings and reading the earnest thank-you notes to Pop, who smiled and laughed, saying, "That's just wonderful. I can't believe how well those little kids can write!"

As soon as we finished going through the letters, we still had a couple of hours to go, and Pop returned to his seat next to the pilot. I tried to read, but felt drowsy as I leaned against the window.

When I opened my eyes, my view of the dry, dusty land outside my window was about to turn to water as we reached the coast of the Gulf of Mexico. I leaned across the aisle of the Pilatus to sneak a peek at Pop. Backlit by the late afternoon sunshine pouring through the cockpit window, I could see that, no, Pop was not asleep. He would occasionally turn his head and mouth words to Jason, and I could even make out a smile. He was enjoying every second of this adventure.

We landed well after dark and disembarked, tired but elated. John, attentive to every detail, had arranged for a rental car to meet us at the small airport, and it was a short drive to food and lodging. After a burger and a beer at the nearby Applebee's, I checked into my room, took a quick shower, and did a belly flop on to the bed. It had been a very long, stimulating day. Too exhausted to read and too excited to sleep, I made a cup of chamomile tea and turned on the television. Within moments I fell into a deep sleep. It seemed like barely twenty minutes later when I was jolted awake by a loud rapping on the door.

"Sun's up," Pop barked through the door. "You gonna sleep all day?! Let's go, men!" He had no doubt been up since four in the morning, his usual waking time, waiting impatiently for all of us to get up, have breakfast, and get moving.

Fantasy of Flight Air Museum—the name could not be more apt. Tucked between two shimmering blue lakes, the massive museum has several grassy landing-strips and numerous buildings and hangars. The huge parking lot was empty. At that time, the museum was closed to the public, so we were the only guests in the entire complex. As we drove through the front gate and made our way alongside the maze of buildings and hangars to the main entrance, there seemed to be colorful birds, large and small, everywhere.

The Florida sun was heating up, and it was pleasant to get out of the SUV and stretch our limbs in the warm, humid air. As we approached the front doors, impressively designed in a vintage Art Deco style, Kermit's passion for both planes and poetry was evident in the Mission Statement etched onto the Museum's exterior:

Since the dawn of time...
Man has been fascinated by flight.

That fascination...
Is a physical reflection...
Of what we all long to return to.

We all fly in our dreams...
And when we awake...
We long for that inner freedom.

I hope...
The fantasy of flight...
Will help light that spark within...
To continue you on your journey.

We've seen...
The last 100 years...
Let's create the next.

Flight...
More than anything else on this planet...
Symbolizes man's desire to go beyond himself.

Let's use it...

To inspire mankind...
To take the next step on its journey.

Eager to take advantage of the early morning light, videographer Bryan immediately began to assemble a portable drone for some aerial footage of the museum as the rest of us were led into the building to a large reception room.

"It will be only a moment," we were told by a smiling young woman at the front desk. "Would you like some tea while you're waiting?" Pop was offered a chair while Jeff, Steve, and I paced about, silently sipping the tea she had brought us. When a door opened behind us, we whirled around, expecting the legendary Kermit Weeks to emerge. Instead, it was a reporter and cameraman from the local television station. Word of this reunion of a veteran World War II pilot and his warbird had gotten out; this was a newsworthy event.

After a few minutes, the long-anticipated moment arrived. Without ceremony, the receptionist led us down a dim hallway and through a door into an immense airplane hangar.

POP REUNITING WITH THE LAST B-26

"Ohhhhh!!!" Pop cried out. "There she is!" Reacting to the sight of the restored Martin B-26 Marauder, he sounded like he was ten years old again with a broad grin to match it. I had expected him to be overwhelmed in the moment, maybe circle the plane slowly, gazing in awe, murmuring some heartfelt words. Instead, he immediately broke away from the group and, with a tap-tap-tap of his cane, made straight for the plane. He clearly intended to board his bomber. My first response was to stop him, or at least slow him down. This aircraft was no modern jumbo jet with safe jetways, stable handrails, and wide aisles. But there was no stopping Pop from boarding his beloved plane. The only way in was through one tiny hatch underneath the airplane—even a spry young pilot would have to contort his limbs and have the upper body strength to pull himself into the equally small space inside. But a step stool was found, and with a bit of gentle pushing and shoving from us, my father vanished into the belly of the B-26. Seconds later, his radiant face appeared, framed in the cockpit window. He had gone directly to the pilot's seat. I quickly took out my camera and called to him, "Hey, Pop! Give us a thumbs-up!" He raised his thumb and grinned while I snapped a few pictures.

The rest of us, crew and television guys alike, remained outside the aircraft, below my father, allowing him to savor the moment. And savor it he did. He sat in the pilot's seat for about twenty minutes, transported. He wouldn't move. We remained quiet, respecting his moment.

The local news reporters were less patient, and when they could wait no more, they crawled inside to interview Pop. After they got their story, John went next, eager to learn the instrumentation and flight dynamics of the B-26 from one of the few living men who had flown one.

As John came out the hatch, Jeff nodded to me, and I climbed in ahead of him. My first impression was of how dark and cramped the interior was. There was barely any room to move, not that there was anywhere to go, but I made my way through the closet-sized navigation compartment to the cockpit. I poked my head through the little door, and there sat my father, the Pilot.

POP AND TONY IN THE COCKPIT OF THE B-26
AT FANTASY OF FLIGHT

"Sit down," he commanded. He was talking fast, his voice high with excitement. "You've been asking about what it was like to fly a B-26. Let me show you!" Compared to the sterile simplicity of the rest of the interior, the cockpit seemed colorful and beautifully complicated—every square inch of the tiny space was covered with instruments and knobs and levers and pedals, many labeled with indecipherable acronyms.

"Nothing on the B-26 was automated—it was all pilot skill," Pop began. "There was no feathering the prop and gliding into a soft landing like the airplanes today. You had to hit the very front edge of the runway at a steep angle, direct and hard, and then slam on the brakes. If you hit too early, you would crash. If you hit too late you went off the backside and crashed. Either way, you would probably die."

Its beginnings were inauspicious. Sure, the B-26 was fast—powered by two massive Pratt & Whitney R-2800 Double Wasp radial engines, the biggest in WWII. But they didn't quite match the rest of the plane. Her wings were remarkably stubby and thin for an aircraft of its weight. "That's what they said about the bumblebee," Magruder quipped when aviation design experts took one look at the design and declared it would never get off the ground. Indeed, his design resulted in the highest wing loading of any aircraft accepted for service by the Army Air Corps at that time. The term wing loading *refers to the loaded weight of the aircraft divided by the area of the wing. The faster an aircraft flies, the more lift is produced by each unit of wing area, so a smaller wing needs to move faster than a big wing to carry the same weight in level flight. For a pilot, that might be fine when flying at altitude, but the big tradeoff is that it necessitated higher landing and takeoff speeds than most other warbirds. For the B-26, the terrifyingly high 150 mph speed on a final runway approach was understandably intimidating to many pilots, but even a bit slower and the aircraft would stall and crash. Compounding the risk, even at such a high speed, it was imperative for the pilot to get the wheels down on the very front edge of the runway or risk shooting right off the backside. This, after all, was long before the days of spacious runways and computer-controlled navigation systems.*

As I sat beside my father in the co-pilot's seat, he spoke rapidly: "In training we had to learn to do everything with a blindfold on." His hands swarmed expertly over the instruments as he rattled off their functions in detail—elevators, rudder, wing flaps, fuel selector, oil cooler, airspeed indicator, landing gear lever, brakes. On and on. I noticed he didn't mention the bailout bell, which would be used to order the crew to bail out of the airplane. I understood and didn't ask.

"You've got to be able to fly even if you can't see," Pop continued. "What if the cabin filled up with smoke or you were blinded by flak?"

THE COCKPIT OF THE B-26

It had been a long time since I had seen my father so animated. So thoroughly had he internalized the training he received in flying the B-26, that even now, seventy years later, it was as familiar to him as his home computer. His display of knowledge was riveting; I could have sat there listening to him all day, but Jeff was waiting behind me in the dark. Rather than squeeze past him and back into the navigation compartment, I thought it might be interesting to see what it was like inside the nose cone, so I bent forward and squirmed down through the narrow gap.

I immediately wished I hadn't.

Skinny as I am, I could barely fit through the crevice. And once I was inside the nose cone, even with the Browning machine gun having been removed, there was barely enough space to move my body. Squatting in this tiny transparent bubble was no Disneyland ride. I felt trapped, fully comprehending that there was no way out unless the co-pilot, in this case Jeff, climbed out of his seat and exited the cockpit. Trying to stay calm, I stifled a genuine urge to scream. I closed my eyes. What, I couldn't help thinking, must it have been like, to be in this same nose cone, 12,000 feet in the air over enemy territory, faced with bursts of shells erupting from attacking enemy fighters and a constant barrage of flak, the sky turning dark as every concussion shook the airplane, rattling violently as bits of flak sprayed the plane. Hunched over, eyes closed, I could only shudder.

I crouched there, claustrophobic, while I waited, perched on the verge of downright panic, for Jeff to finally get out of the co-pilot's seat so I could squeeze out of what felt like my tomb, scramble through the hatch, stand on solid ground, and breathe some fresh air.

I have never been so happy to be off an airplane in my life.

A long time passed before Pop's head disappeared from the window of the pilot's seat, and we saw his hand waving for us to help him out the bottom hatch. No need of a parachute this time. My brother and I had the privilege of gently assisting him out of his B-26 and onto the hangar floor.

"I could have sat there forever," he told us, his wide grin now a rueful smile. "I really could have."

As it was still early, we were offered a tour of the museum before lunch. After sitting so long in his airplane, it was nice for Pop to stretch his legs, and a great relief for me. The vast collection of vintage aircraft was astounding, each plane apparently restored to its original glory. But truthfully, we strolled around the museum looking at the antiques without really seeing them, too preoccupied to give them the full appreciation they deserved. Fatigued from the long flight the day before and wiped out from the emotional morning, we were in a daze.

After the tour, we returned to the B-26 hangar, where a table had been set up for us under the airplane's wing, and we sat down for a long, pleasant lunch, preceded by a toast to my father and his warbird.

We had just finished dessert when Kermit Weeks strode into the room. I had expected to see him earlier, and in the excitement of the day I had forgotten all about him. Though I had never seen him, I knew instantly that this man was the legend himself. He had the courtly manner, confident gait, and candid smile of an old-fashioned country gentleman. Stepping up to my father, he shook hands, saying, "I'm so sorry to interrupt, sir, but I wanted to introduce myself. I'm Kermit."

Pop looked up from his chair and faltered, trying to find the right words. He seemed nearly in tears.

"Oh, I... I just want to say, thank you so much... I really...," he began.

Kermit smiled, touching Pop's shoulder and shaking his head.

"Oh, it's nothing, really. I'm just so glad I could help reunite you with your aircraft. And I want to thank you, sir, for your service."

With that he turned and briskly strode off, leaving us to enjoy this extraordinary occasion.

After lunch, there was still more to do. All this time, Bryan had been shooting footage of the event. Now it was time to put a face to the story. He asked my father if he could interview him, away from the group and excitement. Although Pop usually shunned attention of any kind, he graciously agreed.

Jeff took me aside, saying, "Pop's gonna be busy for a while, let's go explore!"

While researching the museum, I hadn't gotten around to studying its layout or the extent of its exhibits. And since we were the only visitors inside this treasure trove of aeronautic history, it was a unique opportunity. We were immediately drawn to Fantasy of Flight's "Immersion Experience," where we first entered a simple space with a wooden floor and benches, a realistic representation of a World War II briefing room. On the walls were mission maps and enemy aircraft recognition posters. Once we sat down, we were transformed into bomber pilots, sitting in on a pre-mission briefing, delivered by a commanding officer silhouetted against a movie screen. His briefing was interspersed with period footage of actual bombing missions and the chatter of our fellow pilots. Once the briefing concluded, we exited into the next immersion room.

This huge, darkened room depicted a winter evening on an airfield during World War II, complete with ground vehicles and outbuildings amid a dim, snowy forest with chirping birds and a gentle breeze. The effect was stunning. But not as stunning as the center piece of the immersion exhibit: an actual, full-sized Boeing B-17 *Flying Fortress*, ready to board. I had to step back to take her in. This was one massive airplane. Designed in 1934, the B-17 was the first bomber to use four engines. Its nickname, *Flying Fortress*, stemmed from the thirteen .50 caliber machine guns that seem to stick out of the aircraft at every angle. We boarded via a set of stairs on the aft side hatch in the tail and exited near the nose of the aircraft. In between we were treated to an astonishing diorama. Mannequins of the ten crew members manned each combat station, each wearing supplemental oxygen masks and dressed in heavy jackets to protect them from the freezing temperatures at altitudes of up to 35,000 feet. Unlike modern airplanes, this warbird had no insulation, no heaters, and no cabin pressurization. There wasn't even a toilet. The sounds we heard that accompanied the vibrations inside the fuselage had been recorded inside a genuine flying B-17. Amid the roar of the engines, we could make out the sharp rattling of machine guns firing and interphone chatter throughout the airplane. We came to a catwalk over the bomb bay where a movie screen showed archival footage of the bay doors opening, bombs falling, and the explosions below. During the war, these real bombs had fallen on real people.

When we stepped out of the B-17, we found ourselves back at the air base in the forest, with mannequin mechanics working maintenance on the airplane. It was easy to believe Kermit's observation that many a B-17 veteran has come out of this exhibition quite overcome.

Near dusk, we took one last look at the B-26 before piling back into the SUV. Lost in thought, we rode back to the motel in silence. I'm sure I wasn't the only one of us who was exhausted. After months of planning and fretting and anticipating, the adventure seemed to be over in just an instant. It was hard to absorb all of what had just happened. I looked over at Pop in the passenger seat, a little concerned. If I felt totally overwhelmed, what must he be feeling? His head was slumped back against the headrest, eyes closed, looking very much like other times I had observed him, fast asleep, in his chair at home or during our sojourns to Jeff's or right after a big dinner. With one significant difference. He was smiling.

Later, alone in my motel room, I collapsed onto my bed, and stared at the ceiling for twenty minutes. I was just beginning to doze off when once again there was a loud rapping on the door. This time it was my brother-in-law, Steve.

"Hey! Come to my room. Quick!" he called, before I could even open the door. I bolted outside, around the corner and through his open door. There, I found Steve, Jeff, and Pop standing in front of the television, smiling and laughing. There were back slaps and high fives all around as we watched the Polk City local news segment spotlighting Pop's reunion with the B-26. Seeing my father as the star of this human-interest story seemed like the perfect finale to the adventure. My heart swelled with pride. After the months of planning, all the hopes and fears and expectations, we had pulled it off. It seemed to me that everything had gone perfectly, beyond anything I could have hoped for, and at this moment my father was truly a happy man.

Mission accomplished.

POP'S FLORIDA CREW: JASON, TONY, JEFF, STEVE, JOHN, DAVE

My father's fifteen minutes of fame continued the following morning when we all went to breakfast at Cracker Barrel before reboarding the Pilatus for the long flight home. As we sat with our stacks of pancakes and mugs of coffee, an older couple came up to our table, timid as mice, and stood beside my father. At first, they just stood there, smiling at him, the man clutching a ball cap in his hands while the woman pulled a handkerchief out of a quilted purse.

"We are so sorry to interrupt," the lady said softly, in a charming Florida accent. "We hate to intrude. But we saw you on the news last night, and we just wanted to tell you how touched we were."

The man nodded, adding, "After watching your reunion with a B-26, we just had to say thank you, sir, for telling your story. I can only imagine being a young man with all that horsepower and all that stress on missions. Then having your freedom taken away so young, as a POW."

We all looked at Pop, afraid that he might be embarrassed. "Well, thank you," he said, with a modest little smile.

"No, thank *you*, sir," the man said. "You are a great American. Thank you for your service."

"God bless you," the lady added.

And before Pop could say another word they turned and tiptoed off.

It was windy and cold in Prescott when we landed at our homebase late in the evening. After unloading, we waited in the dim hangar while the crew tucked in the Pilatus. A side door opened, and woman walked in. When she and Dave embraced, I realized that she must be Francoise, the teacher of the schoolchildren who had written the thank-you notes. In conversation during our trip, Dave had mentioned that his wife was originally from Belgium. I walked over and introduced myself.

"So nice to meet you, Francoise!" I said. "I wanted to thank you for sending the letters and drawings from your students. Pop was really tickled when we read them to him."

"My pleasure!" she replied. "It is my privilege to teach children the importance of honoring the soldiers who risked their lives for us. In Belgium, we are still very grateful to America for helping to liberate our country from the Nazis."

I was curious about Belgium. I love everything about travel—tasting the food, experiencing the culture, and especially meeting the people. And while I had once been to France on business, most of my recreational travels had been to places I considered more "exotic," or what I perceived as maybe more challenging.

But *Belgium*? My vague impression was of chocolate, waffles, and maybe some windmills. Even as I stood there, assuming that Belgium was probably a quaint little European country full of museums and tourist traps, I suspected that I was wrong. Knowing practically nothing about Belgium, I tried to picture it on a map. It's near France, I thought. On long road trips, Lo and I would listen to Agatha Christie mysteries, read by David Suchet, the actor who famously played Hercule Poirot for years on television. The Belgian sleuth was always correcting people who assumed he was French.

"So," I smiled, "In sixty seconds or less, what can you tell me about Belgium?"

"Oh!... *Belgium!*" she smiled back. I could see that this was a topic she needed much more than sixty seconds to talk about.

"Belgium is *so* beautiful! And the people there are so nice—they really *care* about each other. And they *love* Americans. They never forgot World War II, and everyone is still very grateful for what America did. You would be treated as family. Especially if they knew about your father. And the churches and the museums and the parks and the canals! You *have* to see them! So much history," she beamed.

"What about the food?" I asked, still thinking that Belgium couldn't be all that exciting.

"Oh, the food, the *food!*" she gushed. "You would love the *frites* and the mussels and the croquettes. And all the baked goods are wonderful, and everything is so fresh and delicious. The chocolate is famous, of course. And Belgian beer is the best in the world!"

I had to admit, that last part piqued my interest.

"Have you seen the film *In Bruges*?" she said suddenly.

"No, I haven't seen that one," I said. "Is it a documentary?"

"No, but it will show you what I mean," she insisted. "You should try to see it sometime. And you really must visit Belgium someday," she concluded.

I smiled and politely nodded, still thinking that it was very unlikely I would ever visit Belgium.

CHAPTER 3

Time's Up

You could leave life right now. Let that determine what you do and say and think.

—Marcus Aurelius

The next day, I was once again on an ordinary commercial jet, flying back to California, and I had time to decompress and reflect on Pop's reunion with the B 26. It had been gratifying to see my father being celebrated and actually enjoying himself. "I was no patriot," he usually insisted. "I just always wanted to fly airplanes. I had to fly."

Not believing he had done anything special, he did not want or expect to be thanked for his service. He maintained that he had been proud, not of himself, but of being a part of something bigger than just himself.

"I wasn't the only one," he would say.

I thought about my brother Bill, wishing he could have been with us on this trip. For much of his life, he had been kind of a rolling stone, but after years of moving around, trying new things, he and his wife had settled down near our parents in Sun City West. Before he got cancer, Bill had been devoted to them, driving them to appointments, doing chores, and just spending time together. In the wake of this great loss to our family, I had decided to be more attentive to my parents. I couldn't replace my brother, but I wanted to do more than talk on the phone and squeeze in occasional visits.

At the San Francisco airport, I boarded the Sonoma County shuttle and settled in for the long drive to Santa Rosa. I had always been proud of Pop. He was, after all, my father. I thought about the nice old couple in the Cracker Barrel who just wanted to tell him that they were proud of him, too. I thought about John. Not so long ago, John had also been a stranger. It was amazing to me—just a few months ago, after an evening's conversation with my father, John had offered to sponsor this chance for Pop to show his boys the airplane in which he had flown and fallen. It was slowly dawning on me that Pop's experiences were important, not just to me, not just to my family, but to people in general. I had a vague idea that I needed to do something about it.

A few months after our trip to Florida, I received an all-caps email from Jeff with a *YouTube* link. I clicked on it, and there was a picture of my father, giving a thumbs-up from the pilot's seat of the B-26. The title of the video: *REUNITED—P.O.W. and The Last B-26.*

I must have watched it seven times that day. And I must have sent the link to about twenty of my friends. After getting home and back to my routine, I had forgotten all about the videography, so seeing the film was quite a thrill. When I called Pop, he told me that Bryan had visited him a few weeks after the trip to get the final scene. Since then, Bryan had edited several hours of footage into a coherent short film. In less than ten minutes, he had captured a revealing glimpse into my father and his experience. After being posted for only a few weeks, the video already had scores of views. Sometime later, Jeff emailed me another link, an announcement from the local newspaper announcing its picks for the year's best films:

Best Documentary: *REUNITED—P.O.W. and The Last B-26*
Director: Bryan Matuskey
Country: U.S.
Running time: 9:30

In this incredibly inspiring true story, you will hear Barney Wasowicz, a B-26 Marauder pilot in WWII, honor his fellow Prisoners of War by sharing his story on being shot down by a FW190 over occupied France, living for 16 months as a P.O.W., and being reunited with North America's only intact B26—the plane that saved his life.

The film was certainly moving. People responded to it. And yet, for me it seemed like the well-crafted trailer of a full-length feature film that had yet to be produced. It established the premise for a story, raising more questions than it answered.

I knew the synopsis: As a young man during World War II, my father enlisted in the Army Air Corps; he learned to fly; he went overseas to England; he flew seventeen missions; he was shot down during his eighteenth mission; he was captured by the Germans; he spent sixteen months in a POW camp. And then he came home, married my mom, worked for the Detroit fire department, had five kids, and lived happily ever after. But what about the rest of the story? What was it *like* to go to war? What was *he* like in those days?

The war was always in Pop's rearview mirror, but he wasn't looking back. "Always forward; never back," he liked to say. When I was born, the last of those five kids, my father was in his mid-forties, and still looking ahead. Life with the family was his adventure, full of road trips all over the United States, waterskiing excursions in his handmade boat, and a midlife decision to leave the Polish neighborhood in Detroit and move out west.

Now that Pop was in his nineties, I realized that once he was gone, the past would be all that was left. And I didn't even know the whole story.

It seemed like I should already know the details of my father's years as a bomber pilot and POW; on the other hand, I realized that it was a typical situation. Like many of his cohort, my father had never been one to talk about the war, or even look at old photos. A portrait hanging in the house of him in his bomber jacket was as familiar as the rest of the furniture, but not a topic of conversation.

As a kid, I loved watching old war movies like *The Great Escape* on television. But on such occasions, Pop would find something else to do, so I would try to get my mother to talk about Pop and the war.

"Ask your father," she would say.

I never had. Although I was the youngest, I knew that my older brothers and sisters had not heard many war stories either. It was understood: Pop had put the war behind him. Never demonstrative, always self-effacing, he was a quiet man with a deep-seated aversion to self-aggrandizement.

And yet.

According to Mom, Pop had always wanted to "make his mark." One thing was certain, the story of my father's service could not be told in ten minutes. I began to think that I should be the one to ask, to listen, to understand. And to write it all down. There was still time.

✈ ✈
✈ ✈
✈ ✈

Time waits for no man.

Four years passed. Over a hundred thousand people had viewed the video of my father boarding the last Martin B-26 Marauder. The hundreds of comments from viewers extolling my father's virtues had brought tears to my eyes and resolve to my mind. But while my regular visits to my parents had gone on as usual, my design to learn more about Pop's war service seemed to fade, lost in the more pressing needs of our reunions: exchanging news, doing errands and chores, and driving hours to visit Jeff and his family. For a while it seemed as if these rituals would go on forever. I had always kidded Mom and Pop about their amazingly active retirement. "Another cruise?" I would say. "When are you two going to slow down?" Of course, they did slow down, gradually. Still, it was not until they were in their nineties that they moved into assisted living. After that, they didn't want to go anywhere, not even to Jeff's. They just wanted to sit and listen to me talk about my life. And then Mom got cancer.

Like my brother Bill's, my mom's battle with cancer had been short and intense. It had happened so fast—even at ninety-three, my mom was still one of the most energetic people I'd ever known. But cancer strikes with devastating quickness. I could hardly believe she was gone. My parents had been married seventy-two years, and now suddenly Pop was alone.

As a celebration of life service for my mother concluded, family and friends proceeded out of the Chapel of the Valley. In the twilight, the small, warm church glowed like a little cottage in a fairy tale, its stained-glass windows lit up from within. It was mid-December, the beginning of winter, and here I was again, saying goodbye to another member of my family at Christmastime. I shivered in my new gray suit, my arm around my wife. Standing on a hilltop to the west, silhouetted against the last faint rays of the setting sun, a man in a kilt played bagpipes. The sound of the plaintive pipes was heartbreaking. I looked around for my father. He stood alone, leaning against the back wall of the chapel. He looked small. He could still walk, with a cane, but not too far. Virtually blind, he could not see the figure on the hill, but he surely could hear the steady thrum of "Amazing Grace," echoing across the brown hills of Prescott Valley.

I stepped toward him, but hesitated. What could I say to a man who had just lost his beloved wife of seventy-two years? True, I was grieving the loss of my mother, but I was not facing life without my co-pilot. To be ninety-six years old, robbed of his vision by macular degeneration, and now deprived of his lifelong partner, he must have felt more than bereaved. His friends from the old days were long gone. His children led their own lives, in different cities. He had lived a long, full life. What did he have to look forward to now?

"I never thought it would end this way," he told me later. "First Bill and now your mother. Why am I still here?"

He didn't have to explain. Of course, no one would have said as much, but most of the family had assumed that my father would go first. He had always slept badly, waking up every hour or so. He often had nightmares about bailing out of a burning airplane. He endured chronic backaches and headaches, fried everything in gobs of butter, and kept to himself. Almost four years Pop's junior, Mom had always seemed even younger. Exuberant and vivacious, she walked daily, led water aerobics for fellow seniors, volunteered at the church. And she kept in touch with dozens of family members, calling on the telephone, sending cards, and visiting as often as possible.

After the memorial service, family members from near and far gathered at Jeff's home. Before dinner, Pop pulled my siblings and me aside, and with warm words and wet cheeks presented each of us with a generous check. It was from Mom, he told us. She had saved it over the years and set it aside as a parting gift to her children. There was a catch: We were to spend the money on something we really wanted but didn't think we could afford. She wanted us to have a bit of "crazy money." She wanted us to remember her by enjoying ourselves.

Sitting with my father after dinner, I struggled to keep up the conversation. Pop had never been much of a talker. Mom had been the conversationalist— whether in person or on the telephone, she was always prepared with a series of questions: "Anything new at work? What's going on in the garden? How are the dogs? Any new projects on the house?" She would want to know every detail, never tiring of our conversation. And she was particularly interested in what we were doing for fun—what did we do on the weekend, where did we dine, what vacation plans did we have. "Make sure you get out and *do* things," Mom would say. "Don't wait. Travel, see the world. Do it before you get old and can't do anything anymore."

Words to live by.

Mom would finish her conversation and then hand the receiver to Pop: "Come on, Barney, just say *hello*." Although he certainly cared about his children's lives, he seemed to prefer hearing the details later from Mom. Mostly, he cared about our financial stability. "How's work?" he would ask. "Interest rates are going down again. Are you thinking of refinancing your house?" I wondered what else we would talk about now that Mom was gone.

When the memorial was over, we said goodbye, and once again, I went back to my life in California. I could imagine what my father's life was going to be like. At Silver Springs, the assisted-living community where he and Mom had lived for just a couple of years, Pop followed a simple routine. In the morning, he would slide the daily menu list under his table-top magnifying reader to plan what he would order. Between meals, he would return to the reader to check the mail and sort through his bills and investment statements. After lunch he might put on an audiobook and fall asleep in his recliner while listening. He would watch the news every evening and find it depressing. He'd long had a keen interest in computers, and at one time had spent hours a day on his projects; for years he was on call teaching computer basics to fellow seniors and trouble-shooting their technical issues. But as his vision deteriorated, it became too difficult to navigate the keyboard or see the tiny figures on the screen, so his beloved Macintosh sat gathering dust.

I called him often, but after I gave him my updates, there wasn't much to talk about. He started saying, "Thanks for calling," something he had never said when Mom was alive. Without my mom there to keep the conversation going and devise outings and chores for us to do, I supposed my next visit with Pop would be challenging for both of us.

Then I had an idea. I was excited to call my father because I had what I thought was an interesting topic for him.

One evening after dinner, Lo was looking for something to watch on Netflix. "How about this?" she said. "It's called *In Bruges*."

"Bruges?" I said. "What's that?"

"It's a city in Belgium," Lo said. "I read about this one in *The New Yorker* a while ago. Kind of a surreal black comedy."

About twenty minutes into the movie, I realized why it sounded so familiar. It was the film that Francoise had mentioned to me four years ago when she was rhapsodizing about Belgium in the airplane hangar. If the cinematography was to be believed, Francoise had not been exaggerating. Both Lo and I decided then and there that we had to see this little country for ourselves.

"It's a cool movie shot in Belgium," I told Pop on the phone. "And guess what? Lo and I have decided what to do with Mom's money—we're planning a vacation to Europe. In a few months we're flying to Amsterdam to kick it off!" His response floored me.

"Amsterdam?" he laughed. "Then you'll be flying into Schiphol Airport. I bombed that airport. My most dangerous mission."

"You *what*?" I was stunned. What a bizarre coincidence. Suddenly speechless, I forgot about our vacation and began to think about my father. How was it that I knew absolutely nothing about his bombing of Schiphol Airport during World War II? I always assumed that his "most dangerous mission" had been the one in which he was shot down and captured by the Germans. And had it really been four years ago that I thought there was still time to ask Pop about the war? I was supposed to be the one to ask, to listen, to understand. It was at that moment, right then and there, on the phone, that I made a vow to write it all down. When we had gone to Florida and reunited Pop with the B-26, I promised myself that I would ask him to tell me more about his service, especially his sixteen months in a German prison camp. Once I had returned home to my everyday life, I promptly forgot about this promise. Now here I was, realizing once again that a large portion of my father's life was a mystery to me. Once again, on the phone with him, I felt that it was vitally important that I ask him to tell me about what he'd experienced.

"Hello? Tony? Are you still there?"

"Yes, I'm here!" I said, snapping to attention. "I'm just surprised. I don't remember hearing about that mission."

"Well," he said, "Maybe that's because I never told you about it."

"Pop?" I began, "Next time I visit, let's sit down and talk about your experiences during the war, okay?"

After I hung up the phone, I went to the computer and called up the video of my father reuniting with the B-26. Curious, I scrolled through some of the comments. People from all over the country were showering my father with admiration and gratitude. One comment caught my attention. The writer stated, "*That was nice to hear from someone who flew in World War II. Soon there will be only a few left. Think the young children should learn about our country's history from a real hero.*"

I faced the facts. Time was running out. The stories had to be told, and I couldn't stand around waiting for someone else to listen and record them. By some miracle, at ninety-six, Pop was reasonably healthy and still in possession of his faculties. I had gambled with fate long enough. Pop's legacy was in my hands, and I wouldn't let him down. The few war stories I had heard as a child growing up, I had mostly forgotten. But now I felt a sudden, inescapable calling: I resolved to capture every detail that he could tell me and pass it along to future generations. My mission was now clear.

A month or so later, I arrived at Silver Springs Assisted Living for my regular visit to my father, well after suppertime. Exhausted by the stress of traveling, preoccupied with my own concerns, and missing my mom, I wasn't feeling too talkative. I was afraid that it was too late, that Pop would prefer not to talk about it, that he was too tired, or that he just didn't remember it anymore. It would have been easy to turn on the television and call it a night.

But when he opened the door to his apartment, my father looked alert and refreshed.

"Wow, you look great, Pop!" I said truthfully. "What the heck have you been doing?"

"I stopped taking all those pills," he admitted dryly.

"Nice work!" I said. After my mom's memorial service, he told me and my siblings that he was going to go off his meds—"to hasten my death," he said— and while everyone else had reluctantly agreed, I was enthusiastic about the plan. Not because I wanted to "hasten his death," but because I believed that he would feel better. The meds were the usual regimen of pharmaceuticals meant to "support" the aging bodies of people whose only malady was being old. I had either forgotten or didn't really believe he was going to stop the meds right away.

Ironically, quitting the pills seemed to have the opposite effect.

"You look better than you have in years!" I said.

"I know! I feel great. But my plan backfired. I don't want to feel great. I just wanted to die sooner."

Once I had settled in, I brought up the war. I reminded him (and myself) that I wanted to sit down and ask him about his war-time experiences. I wanted to write a small book, I said, and I wanted him to start from the beginning and tell me everything—from his flight training in the Army to his imprisonment in a POW camp. I had imagined I would have to do some clever convincing to get him to say anything, so his response surprised me.

"Well, what do you want to know?"

A lifelong coffee drinker, Pop had recently switched to green tea, so I made two cups, and I dug out my notebook and pen. At first, he didn't have much to say, rolling his hazy eyes every time I asked him to recall what was ancient history to him. But as I pressed on, he warmed to the idea of talking about the war. Maybe the firing of the awakened neurons in his brain felt good. And I think he came to realize that this was his last chance. If he wanted to say anything, now was the time. And he remembered much of it with astonishing clarity. I took notes late into the night.

Over the next few months, whether in person or on the telephone, I continued to draw him out, eventually accumulating several notebooks filled with my scribbled notes. Often times Pop seemed to be humoring me, but he would patiently go over the stories, old to him, but new to me, in minute detail. The sharpness of his mind and memory impressed me. Still, sometimes he would frown and laugh at me, saying, "Now how on earth could I remember that detail? That was seventy-five years ago!"

What started as a little chat over a cup of tea turned into several months of "interviews." Every time we talked, I sat with my pen and notebook and peppered Pop with questions, pressing him for more detail.

"I suppose I should begin this story with how and why I ended up in the U.S. Army Air Corps," Pop began.

It all started with a little boy's passion for airplanes.

CHAPTER 4

Learning to Fly

I've been where you are now and I know just how you feel. It's entirely natural that there should beat in the breast of every one of you a hope and desire that some day you can use the skill you have acquired here. Suppress it! You don't know the horrible aspects of war. I've been through two wars and I know. I've seen cities and homes in ashes. I've seen thousands of men lying on the ground, their dead faces looking up at the skies. I tell you, war is Hell!

—General William T. Sherman

"It was never a question," my father told me when I asked how he got into World War II. "I always dreamed that someday I would be a pilot. Not just a pilot, but an *Army* pilot."

While just a small child, Pop developed a passion for airplanes. Some might say an obsession. His very earliest memories, around five years old, were of staring at picture books of cartoon airplanes of all sorts and colors. Crayons in hand, he constantly drew pictures of airplanes, played pilot and, of course, watched with rapt attention as he saw aircraft fly across the sky over his head. Seeing the occasional war film at the local movie theater further imprinted the images on his psyche. As he grew older, he would spend hours designing and building model gliders out of paper and cardboard and painting them in realistic detail.

Childhood passed, but my father's dream of flying stuck. During the Great Depression, the only way to fly airplanes in the Army was to join the United States Army Air Corps. Created after the United States entered World War I in April 1917, the Air Corps was basically the precursor to the U.S Air Force. By the late 1930s, American air power lagged far behind both Britain and Germany. As tensions began to rise in Europe, it was apparent that the aircraft fleet and its personnel needed to be modernized, quickly.

"The war in Europe was getting to the point where we would probably have to get involved," Pop explained. "This meant that a lot more pilots would be needed, and the restrictions would have to be lowered."

When my father graduated from high school in 1940, the requirements to join the Air Corps were a college degree and a minimum age of twenty-and-a-half years old.

"After I finished high school," Pop continued, "I enrolled in night school at Lawrence Institute of Technology to study Mechanical Engineering. My intention was to get a degree and then join the Air Corps."

Also working at an aluminum company during the day, he was driven by a single goal—do whatever was necessary to get up in the air.

By 1941, the war in Europe was raging; even before the attack on Pearl Harbor, it seemed inevitable that the U.S. would have to join the cause. Now that more pilots were needed, the requirements were altered, lowering the minimum age, and eliminating the need for a college degree.

"During my first year of college, I discovered that the Army had created a new position called *Flight Officer*," Pop told me.

To qualify for this new rank, a recruit simply needed to be nineteen years old, join the Army, and score reasonably well on an IQ test. The window suddenly open, Pop quit night school and leaped through.

Two of the three requirements were easy for Pop: He was nineteen years old, and when he took the requisite IQ test, he scored an impressive 142 (IQ classification scales differ by the individual test but by any standard this is in the top rank level of "Extremely High" or "Very Gifted").

"I did have one problem," he admitted. "In order for me to volunteer for Army service, I needed my mother's permission and signature, which I knew I would never get."

My grandmother—Babcia—was terrified of airplanes, and she did not want her only son flying one into combat.

"So what did you do?" I asked.

"I forged her signature on the application and never told her that her permission was required."

"*You?*" I said, in disbelief. "*You* forged Babcia's signature?" At first, the notion of my father misleading his own mother surprised me. Soon, however, I saw that, as with many young men, flouting authority had been a trend with him.

He enlisted in October 1941, just a couple of months before the Japanese attack on Pearl Harbor.

POP IN PRE-FLIGHT TRAINING

Now that he was eligible to join the Air Corps, my father's dream of flying military aircraft was becoming a reality. The following months were a whirlwind of schooling—imagine preparing a raft of twenty-year-old kids to fly airplanes in combat. Pop was sent to Keesler Field at Biloxi, Mississippi, for airplane mechanics training.

"As soon as I was able to, I submitted my application for pilot training in this new program," Pop continued. "The application was accepted a couple of months later, and I was ordered to take a very strict physical exam and a written test. I also had to appear before an Officers Board for an oral exam."

"Sounds intense," I said.

"It was," Pop said, "but everything turned out all right, and I was on my way!"

The Army Air Corps was rushing to teach young soldiers how to fly and get them into combat as quickly as possible. In rapid succession, the pilot training program took my father to several different bases: One month at Randolph Field in Texas for Pre-Flight training; three months in Muskogee, Oklahoma, for Primary Training; three months in Brady, Texas, for Basic Training; three months in Lubbock, Texas, for Twin Engine Advanced Training. There he received his wings, graduating as a Flight Officer, the new rank created for men below the age of twenty-one. Finally, still wet-behind-the-ears, my impetuous young father was sent to Avon Park, Florida, and assigned to B-26 Marauder bomber training.

"I was crushed. Very disappointed," he told me.

"Really?" I said.

"I always pictured myself flying a sleek fighter plane, not a big, bulky bomber. But that's what they needed me to do. I had no choice."

Disappointment turned to dread the day my father arrived in Avon Park, when he learned that two B-26s had crashed that very morning, killing all fourteen airmen. The reality check was sobering, but the young men carried on with the business at hand.

"Upon arrival at the training base in Avon Park, the first order of business was forming crews," Pop explained. "Crews that trained together from the beginning learned to work as a team. This way you knew what to expect from each man and they knew what to expect from you. It was a good system. If a member of your crew is sick, you don't fly. The only time a crewmember was replaced was if...." Pop trailed off. He had a forlorn look on his face and his voice changed, slowing, as he looked down.

The B-26 normally had a crew of six. My father was assigned the first pilot position.

He continued, "When the crews were first assembled, my best friend, Jimmy Alexander, was assigned to be my co-pilot."

It was a heart-wrenching story. A few months into their flight training, still in shock over the fourteen dead comrades and others that followed, the young airmen witnessed another tragedy.

"Jimmy felt that he deserved to be a first pilot," Pop went on. "So he complained to the Commanding Officer. The C.O. reviewed his record and changed the assignment, giving him his own crew. We had our Primary Flight Training by the same instructor, and I remember the instructor telling me that Jimmy was one of the few natural born pilots he had ever instructed."

A very short time later, during a training exercise, Jimmy's B-26 spun out of a thundercloud and crashed, killing all onboard. In a grim coda, Pop accompanied his best friend's body to his hometown in Birmingham, Alabama, for burial. The young men had just begun flight training, and already one their most gifted comrades had lost his life.

PRIMARY TRAINING CREW

"The B-26 was an unforgiving airplane, and it was killing pilots because it never gave them a chance to make mistakes," recalled General Jimmy Doolittle, hands down one of the greatest pilots ever. With luck and an experienced pilot, this bumblebee bomber was an aeronautical marvel. But as the U.S. dove headlong into a World War, the demand for American pilots was high and time was short, and taming this precision machine was not a job for inexperienced young trainees. After entering service with the United States Army aviation units, the aircraft quickly received the nickname "Widow-Maker" due to the high accident rate during takeoffs and

landings. Even off the runway dangers lurked. Her racing wings resulted in a high "minimum control speed," the speed at which an aircraft can lose one of its engines without becoming uncontrollable. And engine losses on B-26s were frequent. The Pratt and Whitney engines were prone to failure, and when an engine failed, the pilot had to maintain a high airspeed, or the airplane would roll upside down and plummet to the ground. During training at MacDill Field, Florida, as many as fifteen B-26s crashed into the sea in a single month, leading to the exaggerated catchphrase, "One a day in Tampa Bay." Other common monikers for the aircraft included "Martin Murderer," "Flying Coffin," "B-Dash-Crash," "Flying Prostitute" (it was very fast and had no visible means of support), and "Baltimore Whore" (a reference to the city where Martin was based).

Undaunted by the fatalities, my father and his comrades continued their training. Eventually, my father fell in love with the B-26: "As I've told you before, the plane had such a bad reputation because it was a difficult airplane to learn to fly," he said. "Once you did learn to fly it, which took about fifty hours in the air, it was a wonderful airplane."

He paused for moment, reminiscing about that brief carefree time during training.

"Before my first in-flight lesson—which was very scary—" Pop continued, "I was required to attend ground school and learn everything about the plane, including pointing to each instrument and control in the cockpit while blindfolded. My first look inside the cabin convinced me that I would never accomplish this."

He did of course master everything about the plane, a skill that he could still demonstrate at the age of ninety-two while onboard the B-26 at Fantasy of Flight. In addition to the countless hours sitting in classrooms and studying books, aspiring pilots had to spend about fifty hours in the air learning to fly the challenging bomber. They constantly practiced all phases of combat flying—formation flying, dropping bombs on dummy targets, skip-bombing, target practice with the .50 caliber machine guns mounted on the airplane, and long-distance cross-country trips.

"Skip-bombing was my favorite," Pop said, smiling broadly.

"What's that?"

"Skip bombing is a practice used in low-level bombing," Pop explained. "You fly in about ten to twenty feet above the ground, fly directly toward the target, such as a building or tank, and release the bomb from fifty to one hundred feet away. The bomb would skip along the ground, like a flat stone skipping on water. You'd watch it skip and then, with any luck, it would land on the target. Because the fuse was in the nose, the bomb wouldn't explode until it hit the target."

"That does sound fun!" I said.

"Oh yeah, it *was* fun! It was one of the exciting parts of our training," Pop recalled.

Sometimes it was, perhaps, a little too much fun. One time, a local farmer angrily reported that one of the pilots had been skip-bombing his cows in a nearby field. It had not been my father who harassed the cows— *this* time; nevertheless, he was the first man called in for questioning by the Commanders.

"Luckily, I was able to prove that I was flying in a different area entirely," Pop said.

It seems my mild-mannered, no-nonsense father had been known as a rebel in his day.

"I know none of you kids would ever believe it," he said with a smile, "but I was considered to be quite the maverick in training camp. I was the cockiest pilot there. The Commanders would call me on the carpet anytime there was a report of any infraction."

This was, indeed, hard for me to believe. I thought of my father as a straight arrow: reserved, moderate, conservative, polite. He was one of the few people I have ever known who had no vices. He never uttered a single swear word, not in my hearing. Not *damn*, not *hell*, much less F-bombs. Nor was he a drinker. I had never seen him tipsy, let alone drunk, not even at the frequent, large gatherings with our fun-loving extended family in Detroit. Although he enjoyed an occasional gin and tonic—*Tanqueray and Schweppes, or nothing, thank you*—one cocktail was always enough. Of course, like just about everyone in those days, he smoked, heartily supported by the U.S. Army. But one day, he and my mom decided to give up cigarettes to save money for their twenty-fifth wedding anniversary trip, and he didn't seem to miss it.

How had this "maverick" Air Corps pilot turned into a paragon of adulthood? Although I never thought to ask him, I suppose that he was the rare apple that does fall far from the tree. I did not personally know my grandfather—my namesake Antoni died in 1941—but I did know that, even during the Depression, he had made a relatively good living as a brick mason. A master of the trade, he belonged to the union, and wages were high. The family lived in a nice brick house. Every Saturday, Babcia and my Aunt Wanda would hustle the males out of the house so that they could spend all day tidying and scrubbing the house from top to bottom. My father was given money to go to the movies. As for Antoni, there may have been another reason he would leave the house on Saturdays.

Antoni, having worked quietly and skillfully at his trade all weeklong, would suddenly become a gregarious barfly on payday. According to family lore, every Friday, my grandfather would take his paycheck to the local bar where he would expend a large portion of his hard-earned money buying drinks for friends, strangers, and of course, himself. His misguided generosity made him popular around Detroit, but infuriated his wife, who would sit up waiting to unleash a blue streak of livid Polish profanity at him when he finally staggered home. This pattern of Antoni's self-indulgence and Babcia's verbal abuse seems to have affected my father profoundly. Pop was on the brink of enlisting in the Army when Antoni met his untimely demise. Stumbling on the street, in front of his favorite bar, Antoni was killed after being hit by a car.

Like Antoni, my father had also made a relatively good living, but in most other ways, he seemed to be the opposite: introverted, temperate, responsible, frugal. As a young pilot in the Air Corps, he exhibited a different kind of recklessness. He loved flying and testing the limits of both himself and his airplane.

As I listened to my father's stories about being a bold young man learning to fly, I realized that he had continued being a maverick long after the war. He had settled down, but he did not carry a brand. Both of his parents had been born in Poland, and both clung to the Old-World ways. When the war ended, Pop's first about-face was to leave his roots in the tightly knit Polish neighborhood in Detroit and follow the old romantic notion. He was a young man, and he bought a brand-new car and went West.

"After the war, I had hoped to pick up my life where I left off," Pop recalled. "I soon found out that it wasn't that easy."

Under the GI Bill, he tried studying at an aeronautical school in California, but after about a year, he discovered that the school was nonaccredited, a sham operation taking advantage of the ample government funds. He also went to photography school, which he loved, but he didn't see a career in it. Disappointed, he returned to Detroit, where he worked at the construction company of a distant cousin. As a drafter, he excelled at taking measurements of buildings and drawing them up. But the exacting work was tedious, and Pop was restless. To entice him to stay, the cousin offered to pay Pop's tuition if he wanted to go to architecture school. There was a catch: He would have to repay the cousin by working for the firm. Once again, Pop pulled back.

"I tried various things," he said. "Went into business with your Uncle Hank. Two gas stations. That didn't go well—Hank had a drinking problem. For a while I had my own photography studio. Eventually, I got a job with the Detroit Fire Department, where I was able to use my photography training and work my way up to Inspector and Fire Photographer."

"How did you finally settle on the fire department?" I asked.

"I met your mother!" he said with a smile.

"Go on," I said, even though it was a story I already knew.

"I thought you wanted to hear about the war!" he laughed. "You remember. Uncle Jim and Aunt Wick set us up on a blind date. The Firemen's Ball."

"Sure, I remember. Mom told us that you didn't bring her a corsage."

"She never let me live that down," he said. "Anyhow, her brothers were all in the fire department. Jim suggested I give it a try."

And the rest, as they say, is history. Once Pop found his *co-pilot*, he was ready for take-off.

Even now, at 96, Pop was still an unorthodox, independent-minded person. He chuckled as he recalled his younger self, committing some of his most egregious rule infractions.

"I don't remember why I tried those stunts in a bomber. It probably just seemed like a good idea at the time," he said, shaking his head. "I guess I was like every red-blooded twenty-one-year-old red-hot pilot who had just received his wings. We were yet to learn that this war was not all fun and games."

For a little while, though, flight training was an exciting adventure for the youthful officers.

"One of the things I did learn was why the B-26 was redlined at 350 miles per hour," Pop continued.

On one occasion, perhaps a little resentful about not having been assigned to a fighter plane, my father engaged in some aerial battles at close range. This was strictly forbidden, and for good reason. Dog fighting was extremely dangerous, even for streamlined fighter planes, and never done in heavy bombers, which were not built for such maneuvers. Pop, apparently, wanted to see for himself.

"I tried dog-fighting with a buddy of mine, trying to stay on his tail while he tried to shake me off," Pop began. "In his attempt to lose me, he went into a steep dive. I followed, and while concentrating on his plane, I failed to notice that my airspeed had climbed to 420 miles per hour, way above the redline!"

Again, the maximum safe speed for the B-26 was 350 miles per hour. The controls on the bomber were not power-assisted, and at speeds exceeding 350 miles per hour, the pressure of the airflow over the rudder and elevator surfaces of the wings—theoretically—became impossible to overcome. As they plummeted toward Earth, they frantically resorted to putting their feet up on the control panel for more leverage, and eventually pulled out of the dive with only a few hundred feet to spare.

"It took all the strength my co-pilot and I had to pull the plane out of the dive," Pop concluded.

Then there was the time that, despite aircraft specifications, my father wondered if he could be the first pilot in training to *loop* a B-26. "Out of curiosity," he said.

"Another lesson I learned was that this plane was not designed to fly upside down," he said with a laugh.

He had executed this maneuver numerous times in small single-engine planes that *were* designed for it. Why his crew went along with this idea remains a mystery, but the men securely fastened down all equipment, everybody strapped themselves in, and Pop went for it.

"I dove to pick up speed and attempted this maneuver, which I had performed many times during my pilot training," he told me. "When it reached the top of the loop, it stalled and continued to fall upside down!"

Fortunately, with a lot of skill and even more luck, Pop was able to eventually roll the aircraft upright again and put it into a dive to regain normal airspeed, once again, perilously close to the ground.

"I was able to roll it upright again and dove to pick up normal airspeed!" he said with a grin. "*Luckily*, I had started the loop high enough to do this."

I just shook my head.

There is a portrait of my father wearing his bomber jacket, complete with leather cap, goggles, and white silk scarf. It was one of those things I had seen countless times but had never *looked* at. Now, when I saw his smooth face, smiling rakishly at me across the decades, I gazed back with new interest. He looks scrubbed, young, fresh. And pleased. Once I got used to the idea of my father's having been a *Top Gun* type thrill seeker, I began to wonder how he had gotten away with these dangerous and prohibited stunts. Here he was, twenty years old, a greenhorn in a tightly controlled military training program. Surely the commanders must have had him on their radar, so to speak.

"Oh, they knew about me. At least some of the stuff I did," he admitted. "But I wasn't the only one, you know. I remember once, during a bombing practice run, my new co-pilot, McClanahan, said he would like to try a parachute jump and proceeded to do so, after we dropped our bombs on the target. I had to report by radio when the mission was completed, so I reported '*Mission complete: Dropped ten bombs and one co-pilot.*'"

"That's crazy!" I said, laughing.

"I don't know why, but they didn't think that it was too funny," Pop joked. "We were called in again, and Mac told them he had been standing in the open bomb bay watching the bombs release, when he tripped and fell out. I don't think they believed him, but they dropped it with just a warning."

"That's just crazy," I said again.

"I know," Pop said soberly. "But you have to understand, there was a war going on. These older professional soldiers knew that war was not as glamorous as we kids thought it was."

Demonstrating unexpected empathy, the Army tolerated a fair amount of unorthodox behavior in the young pilots they trained, allowing them to have their fun. The leadership seemed to grasp that these airmen were just children, mere boys who craved adventure without yet comprehending the brutal realities of war. Many of them would go into combat, never to return. Until experienced firsthand, war, combat, and death exist only in the abstract, where they lack real teeth. And, besides, audacity has its place. In time, these thrill-seeking boys would be fighting the Germans, flying dangerous missions while being hammered by enemy fighter planes and intense ground artillery. To prevail, they would need to be more than skillful; they would need to be daring.

CHAPTER 5

Journey to the ETO

Landing in enemy territory: Destroy entire plane, if possible, each plane is equipped with two Thermite Bombs. Set one on top of each wing over main fuel tank, arm the bomb and run like Hell! It will not explode, but in a matter of seconds the mixture of aluminum powder and iron oxide will produce an intense heat of some 4300 Degrees Fahrenheit, which will burn through the wing structure and explode the fuel tanks. If you can't destroy the aircraft, then destroy any secret documents and equipment!

If taken prisoner—give name, rank, and serial number, nothing else.

If you should land in a neutral country, such as Switzerland— destroy secret equipment as you will not be allowed to return to your plane.

Landing at another airdrome in England: Teletype or telephone aircraft designation in code.

If a friendly aircraft is down: Record time seen, place, and altitude observed. Also aircraft type, and other data on success of a crash landing, or number of men seen to bail out.

One last thing, do not wear any clothing on a mission with squadron insignia attached.

—Chester P. Klier, Historian, 386th Bomb Group

After nearly a year of training, my father and his crew had earned their wings: They were ready for active duty. On July 20, 1943, they flew to Waycross, Georgia, where they were issued a brand-new Martin B-26 Marauder; finally, Pop had command of his very own airplane. Having seen his reaction when he was reunited with the B-26 in Florida, I can picture this moment in Georgia: love at first sight.

Pop smiled at the memory, saying, "We had three days to test and break-in this *beautiful* airplane before we delivered it to the base we were assigned to, the 386th Bomb Group, 555th Squadron at Colchester, England."

It would not be an easy beginning. Just getting to the European Theatre of Operations (ETO) would turn out to be a kind of proving ground for the rookie airmen.

The Crewmen Assembled at the Training Base in Avon Park, Florida:

Pilot:	*Barney Wasowicz, aged 20, Michigan*
Co-Pilot:	*Harold McClanahan, aged 21, Indiana*
Bombardier-Navigator:	*Matt Gemery, aged 27, [unknown]*
Engineer:	*Lewis (Bud) Fischer, aged 21, New York*
Radio Operator:	*Bob Carpenter, aged 28, Missouri*
Tail-Gunner:	*Lester Higgins, aged 20, New Jersey*

"It started off pretty easy," Pop remembered. "We were flying over the States. We were excited to finally be on our own, and the views were spectacular. But we were all a little anxious, too—after all, it wasn't every day that a crew of men in their early twenties was given a brand-new half million-dollar airplane with the responsibility of delivering it to England from the U.S."

The first leg on the journey took them from Georgia to Maine. Moments before take-off, my father noticed some men loading boxes onto his plane, a rare exception to the usual strict routine. He soon discovered what the boxes contained: cigarettes. One of the big tobacco companies had supplied the plane with six cases of the prized American drug for free distribution to the troops overseas.

"At the time, I thought it was a very nice gesture on their part," Pop told me with a laugh.

Years later, when he was trying to kick the habit, he was more cynical. He realized that the war had presented a golden opportunity for the tobacco industry: thousands of young men, away from home for the first time, under extremely stressful conditions. Like most of his fellow soldiers, Pop had enjoyed the comfort of free cigarettes, becoming addicted in no time.

The flight to Maine took the crew close to New York City, where my father had cousins. On impulse, Maverick Pop decided to make a little detour to pay them a visit, changing course and heading for the airport.

"Naturally, this was against the rules, so I faked a faulty generator and asked permission to land in the city for repairs. This was granted, and I spent a very pleasant evening and night with my relatives. The rest of the crew found plenty of entertainment in the big city. The next morning—"

"Wait," I interrupted. "You *faked a faulty generator*? And no one raised an eyebrow?"

Pop chuckled. "It did seem like they gave us a lot of leeway, which I am sure would not be the case in peacetime. No, the Army brass didn't question my judgment on having to land in New York—probably because we were on our way to the ETO. Could've been our last hoorah. Anyhow, the next morning, we returned to the flight line and continued on our assigned mission to the base in Maine."

"Unbelievable," I said, shaking my head.

In Maine, after several days of studying the route to England, the crew prepared to fly the first overseas leg of the journey to Labrador, in Canada.

"That flight was somewhat uneventful and so it relieved some of the tension we were all feeling on this totally new experience," Pop recalled. "It was the next leg, the flight to Greenland, that really scared the heck out of us. Flying over land was not a problem as long as the visibility was good. We were supplied with maps and could check our position visually. Flying over *water*, with no visuals—now *that* was a challenge. Navigation was restricted to time, distance, and wind."

I looked up from the dense scribbles of my notebook, puzzled.

"Greenland? What were you doing in Greenland?"

Pop smiled at my question. "Have you ever looked at a world globe?" he asked.

Of course, I had. But it had been a while. In my two-dimensional mind, I pictured an airplane flying due east across the Atlantic Ocean to get to England. But the earth, in fact, is not flat, and in the factual, three-dimensional world, the shortest route from the east coast of North America is in a north-easterly direction. Today, commercial airliners fly from New York to London on a course they call the "Great Circle"—a route which takes them over Boston, along the coast of Maine, and over the edge of south-eastern Canada, before crossing the North Atlantic to the southern tip of Ireland, and then crossing England and touching down in London. Commercial jets fly this course well south of Greenland, simply because they can. Modern aircraft have a range of around 8,000 miles, flying at speeds of up to 550 miles per hour. They also have sophisticated navigation systems, allowing them to fly at night and in virtually any weather conditions. Today, New York travelers can fly non-stop to Heathrow Airport in seven and a half hours.

But this was 1943. The range of a B-26 bomber was less than 3,000 miles, topping out at around 350 miles per hour. Crucially, the crew and the new Marauder lacked sufficient daylight and fuel capacity to go the distance. Those limitations explained the more northerly route required and the multiple stops along the way.

These multiple stops greatly amplified the risk of navigation errors. While a typical jetliner has an advanced global positioning system and over 300 onboard computers to help get from point A to point B, my father and his crew had to rely on maps and hand calculations. Navigation was done by estimating direction, wind speed, and airspeed, and hoping that the airplane ended up at the right spot. This technique was challenging even when the flight was over dry land, and visibility was good, where maps and visual markers could be useful in the navigation. But over long stretches of open water, with no means of rescue, there was no room for error. A crash into the middle of the North Atlantic meant certain death. I shivered at the thought of my father and his crew, crossing the icy sea in this brand new, untested airplane, as they sat strapped into their seats with little to do but hope that their calculations were spot on, and that their complicated new aircraft had no mechanical issues. The one bit of "modern" technology aboard the B-26, the radio, was useless for the trip. Radio signals could easily be picked up by the enemy, so its use was prohibited in those circumstances.

"Anyway, this next leg of our journey proved to be a lot more challenging than flying over the States," Pop continued. "It's funny. Until that trip I actually thought that Greenland was *green*."

I vaguely recalled learning about that irony years ago. In primary school, I was taught that the notorious Viking, Erik the Red, had settled on the continent after being banished from Iceland. He gave it the name *Groenland*, or *Greenland*, as a kind of marketing stunt, to attract settlers to his new, frigid and lonely home. Curious, I later read up on Greenland, and I found the real story is simpler. Recent research reveals that back in 982 A.D., when the Vikings "discovered" Greenland, the grass may in fact have been greener. Scientists examined ice collected from the very bottom of Greenland's glaciers and discovered DNA from various temperate tree species as well as spiders and butterflies. Their evidence suggests that the country was once rich with grass, fields, and forests. At any rate, indigenous Greenlanders, who were never impressed by Erik's real estate campaign, call their country *Kalaallit Nunaat*, which is Inuit for "Land of the People."

Pop continued his story: "The entire island is one huge icecap with mountain peaks jutting out of the snow in some places. All the towns are located on the coastline; there aren't any roads between them. The only access from town to town is by water or air."

"Got it," I said. "The earth isn't flat, and Greenland isn't green."

"You're learning something today!" he teased.

I later learned that Greenland is one of the iciest places on earth. Today, three-quarters of this island country is covered by the only permanent ice sheet outside of Antarctica. Traveling from town to town by sea is dicey at best. On the eastern coast, sea ice forms in vast sheets across the ocean's surface. Some parts will remain frozen all year while other parts break up in summer to form drift ice. At this stage it is constantly on the move, so there is a very real threat of a vessel being trapped, damaged, or driven aground by it. Perhaps even more treacherous are the icebergs shed from Greenland's glaciers. Some are easily as long as an aircraft carrier, and most of the icebergs' mass is below the water surface, making it dangerous for ships to pass them. An iceberg calved from Greenland's *Jakobshavn* Glacier is thought to have been responsible for sinking the Titanic in 1912.

But the sea ice creates hazards in the air as well as in the water.

"Our briefing emphasized paying close attention to our instruments, as altitude was very important," Pop explained. "There wasn't a distinction between the smooth white snowcap and the white horizon, creating a condition called *whiteout*. If you didn't rely on your instruments, you could become disorientated. It's a really weird feeling. It was hard to tell up from down."

Because of the extreme conditions, constant attention to altitude in flight was absolutely critical for pilots. Just before Pop made the journey, several Army pilots had already flown right into the ground, completely unaware that they were too close to the surface of the ice fields.

"The altitude of the snowcap was furnished to us, and we were told to stay at least 500 feet above that," Pop recalled.

Even supposing the crew could find their destination, the final approach was even more daunting. Pop described the airfield: "A short runway with a five-degree incline, located at the base of several mountains which encircled it on three sides. The open side started right on the edge of the water. This runway was at the end of one of the many fjords that led out to the sea. These fjords were like narrow rivers that twisted and turned through the mountains. The only access to the runway was to find the right fjord, drop to about fifty feet above the water ready to land, wheels and flaps down and speed at 145 miles per hour. The fjord we selected would wind its way through the mountains and hopefully end at the runway."

"So, if you chose the wrong fjord, there would be no way to pick up enough airspeed and elevation to get over the mountains?" I asked.

Pop nodded grimly. "At the airbase in Labrador, we were shown a scale model of the fjords and mountains and were told to memorize the shapes of the mountains at the entrance and at the final turn approaching the runway. The one I specifically remember was named 'Sugarloaf Mountain.' This mountain resembled a loaf of bread and when the fjord made about a forty-five-degree turn to the left around this mountain, the runway was right in front of you. The reason we had to fly so low on our approach was that the runway ended at the base of a mountain, and you had to be ready to land as soon as you saw the front edge."

I leaned in as my father relived the intensity of the approach.

"It was imperative that the plane touched down at the front edge of the runway," Pop described. "There would be no second chance; the runway was short, and the mountains steep at the end. I got a quick look at those wrecks at the base of the mountain, and that convinced me that I had better be extra careful on this landing!"

"*Well?* What happened?"

"I'm here, aren't I?" Pop laughed. "We nailed it. Fortunately, everything turned out as planned, and we could breathe again. But that was when it started to dawn on me that this was not fun and games. We were heading to the war zone."

As my father concluded that all had gone smoothly, I felt both relieved and proud, imagining the exhilaration the crew must have experienced, all having proved their mettle that day.

The B-26 had proved its mettle, too.

✈ ✈
✈ ✈
✈ ✈

"Built for speed, highly strung and unforgiving," was how one young pilot described the B-26. The same could said about then Senator Harry S. Truman of Missouri. As the number of crashes in training piled up, he created the Committee to Investigate the National Defense Program to scrutinize military contracts, including Martin's B-26 Marauder. Exactly what motivated Truman is not known. Some claim that the Senator was simply out to get Glenn Martin; but the upshot was that Truman's investigation seemingly forced Martin to modify the aircraft, raised Truman's national profile, and led President Roosevelt to nominate Truman as his running mate in 1944.

After traveling to Baltimore to inspect the Martin plant himself, Truman denounced Martin, the man everyone else seemed to admire. Years after Martin's death, Truman recalled the visit: "Glenn Martin was making B-26 bombers, and they were crashing and killing kids right and left, so I said to Martin, 'What's wrong with these planes?' He said, 'The wingspread isn't wide enough.' So I said, 'Then why aren't you making them wider?' and he said, 'I don't have to. The plans are too far along—and besides, I've got a contract.'"

Truman fumed, "I just don't understand people like that! He was killing kids, murdering kids, and he didn't give a damn!"

But when Truman threatened to void the contract and remove the B-26 from service, the Army Air Corps and Martin fought back. In response to the many criticisms leveled against the bomber, they published lengthy articles to educate the public and defend the B-26 against so-called "slanders." One of the largest of these articles appeared in the May 1944 issue of Popular Mechanics, *which reported that the B-26's aerodynamics had been modified to make it a safer aircraft: Wingspan and wing angle-of-incidence were engineered for better takeoff performance; a larger vertical stabilizer and rudder were created. The new design even enabled the bomber to remain stable while flying on just one engine. This bomber now proved its worth. The bumblebee bomber had its buzz back and was ready to sting.*

WARTIME PROMOTIONAL POSTER

The final two legs of the crew's journey to England were "nothing to write home about," my father told me. "A couple of days in Iceland—*well named!*" he declared— "waiting for the weather to clear, and we were on our way to Scotland."

"Where in Scotland?" I asked.

"Oh, I don't remember the name of the town. We spent an enjoyable evening at a local pub, downing the customary half-pint of ale and playing darts with the natives."

The next morning, they re-fueled and flew the final leg to Colchester, England, their home base. They arrived at the ETO on July 27, 1943. The airbase had been in operation for only about two months, and the 386th Bomb Group had completed only three missions, but the base was humming with activity as soldiers and aircraft were delivered in rapid succession. As everyone was anxiously trying to get "orientated," they realized very quickly the true meaning of *combat conditions*. Their flying skills now thoroughly honed, the men embarked on the final step in their training, four weeks of ground school classes.

"In four weeks, they attempted to teach us everything about this war and what to expect if we were shot down," Pop told me. "In some of the classes, British Intelligence officers briefed us on various methods that both they and the German Intelligence used to obtain information from captured airmen. This information helped prepare me for what was yet to come."

Soon, the drills would be over, their training tested. These young men faced a harsh reality: Some of them, many of them, would prevail, but some would be shot down, and if they were captured, they would need to know what to expect. German Intelligence would be determined to obtain information, so all airmen needed to be conditioned in how to respond. This mental conditioning would be invaluable to my father, who would ultimately face two brutal interrogations after his bomber was shot down.

"We were warned that the German Intelligence was the best in the world," Pop said darkly.

CHAPTER 6

The Food of War

There is only one recipe—to care a great deal for the cookery.

—Henry James

"How's your soup?" I asked my father across the table. I had arrived in time for dinner, and we sat at a table for two in the bright and accommodating Silver Springs dining room. It had the look and feel of an elegant atrium restaurant with high windows, hand-painted murals, graceful chandeliers, white tablecloths, and leather-bound menus. The waitstaff—energetic high school students—bustled about, patiently taking orders and delivering service with a smile. You wouldn't even know you were at an assisted living center. Unless you went into the hallway, which was sort of an ad hoc parking lot for the scooters, walkers, crutches, and canes that were used in getting to the dining room and then decorously left outside the door. At my father's insistence, we had arrived early—"so we won't have to wait in line," he said— but so had everyone else. The trademarked pledge of Silver Springs was "Dine Your Way," meaning, "You can dine early or dine late. Our restaurants are open and ready to serve 12 hours a day." Nevertheless, it seemed that the worst fear of every resident was having to wait to be served. And so, everyone had to wait to be served.

"Pop? How's your soup?" I asked again over the clatter of flatware.

"Not hot enough," Pop answered.

It was a baited question. His food was *never* hot enough. It was kind of a ritual, my asking him. Only rarely could I remember my father lifting a spoon of soup or a cup of coffee to his lips, taking a careful slurp and exclaiming, "Now *that's* hot!" This miracle would usually happen only if he had heated it up himself and begun consuming it immediately. He insisted that the food he ate be excellent. And it had better be hot, too.

My father's preoccupation with food had begun during the war, when he first experienced rationing and shortages. Returning home from Europe, he had a heightened appreciation for food—not just any food, but high-quality, well-prepared, *hot* food. He was raised on steaming platters of Polish classics—*kielbasa*, sauerkraut with beans, pickled pig's feet, *pierogi*, blood sausage, roast duck, stuffed cabbage rolls—and soups. Hearty, hot soups.

It must have been quite a shock to his system when my father found himself at an airbase in England where wartime rationing had been a way of life for years. And it was no wonder that our conversations would often turn to the subject of food, or the lack of it. Before going overseas, he was thrilled at the chance to sample the cuisine in some of the states outside Michigan.

"New Orleans has the best food in the U.S.!" Pop declared.

During his airplane mechanics training in Biloxi, Mississippi, my father had learned a lot about aircraft engineering, but what he recalled most vividly were a few weekends he spent in New Orleans, where a soldier wouldn't need a lot of money to have a good time. As a private in the United States Army, Pop earned a whopping fifty dollars a month. I looked up how much this amount would be in today's dollars and found about $676.51.

"One of the popular songs at that time was 'Twenty-one dollars a day, once a month,'" Pop recalled with a laugh. "After breakfast on payday, we would line up in alphabetical order. The Finance Officer would count out each soldier's pay in cash, deducting laundry and incidentals."

"Incidentals?" I wondered aloud.

"You know, extra expenses, odds and ends. Because my last name began with a *W*, I had to stand in line over four hours. Maybe that's why I hate waiting in lines."

New Orleans was only about a two-hour ride away, and the men got one weekend pass per month. To get to the action, Pop told me, he walked to the nearest road and put his thumb up. The U.S. having recently declared war on Japan, patriotism was surging, so it was simple for a man in uniform to hitch a ride to "The Big Easy."

"*You?* Hitchhiking?" I protested, trying to picture it.

"Sure!" he said smiling. "Hitchhiking to New Orleans was very easy. Except for one time when a guy asked me where I was from. When I said 'Michigan,' he said, 'No damn Yankee is going to ride in my car!'"

In spite of his being a "damn Yankee," my father found the celebrated Southern hospitality on full display in New Orleans. Sponsored by the U.S.O., the United Service Organization, servicemen could go to clubrooms that offered food, dancing, and the opportunity to dine with a local family. At one of those homes, Pop was served a five-course dinner of French cuisine, including wine.

"They had a maidservant, and every time I took a sip of wine, she would refill my glass," he recalled. "When I finally told her I didn't care for anymore, she told me the custom was to put your napkin on the wineglass when you didn't want it refilled." Pop was charmed by this refined gesture, and he never forgot it.

In New Orleans, my father also discovered that he loved trying exotic foods like étouffée, gumbo, and grits. Born and raised almost exclusively on traditional Polish food, he found the new world of Creole cuisine a revelation. These memories of dining in New Orleans were particularly interesting to me. Lo and I had moved to California so that I could become a winemaker and we could really indulge our love of fine food. My father often said that he had no idea where his kids got such "fancy tastes." That was an easy question for me—I got it from my dad.

All my life my parents had made sure that we kids never forgot that they had lived through The Great Depression. We would be having a nice dinner, and Mom would somehow start reminiscing about the bad old days of having to go out in a rowboat with her six siblings to catch bullfrogs and prep them for dinner (her job was to *thunk* them on the side of the boat and snip off their legs with a pair of scissors). Pop, at least, had a gainfully employed father and just one sister, so he was marginally better off. My grandfather proudly maintained the Polish traditions, and Pop remembered Antoni spending hours cutting up cubes of pork, spicing them, and stuffing them through a funnel by hand into pig intestine casings. Half of the attic was filled with hanging sausages, meaty stalactites in various stages of desiccation. And Babcia watched the money like the hausfrau she was. Pop remembered her taking a tin bucket to the butcher every week and demanding he bleed out the living duck directly into her bucket, right before her eyes, so she could make sure she wasn't being cheated.

I had, of course, an inkling about the deprivations Pop had endured in prison camp. But prior to that, I assumed that the U.S. military had seen to it that their soldiers were well fed, even after they were deployed overseas. Pop set me straight.

"There was just no food during the war. For anybody, anywhere. We were always hungry," he stated matter-of-factly.

During his six-month stint at Colchester, England, in 1943, my father witnessed the infamous rationing that Great Britain was subject to during World War II. Prior to Hitler's invasion of Poland, Britain had been importing sixty percent of its food, but now commercial shipping lanes were closed, so precious few supplies were getting through. Not only that, but less food was also being produced in England. When Great Britain entered the war in September 1939, British workers began abandoning farms to join the fight against the Germans. In the first two years of the war, tens of thousands of men joined the cause, letting the fields go fallow. As rationing commenced in January 1940, a small weekly allowance of items like butter and bacon was suddenly the reality.

According to Pop, the men talked of nothing but food. To say that meat was scarce would be a laughable understatement. On the airbase in Colchester, the only real meat the men had, and only occasionally, was a bit of mutton all the way from Australia. Sadly, Pop could never stomach the smell or flavor of even good fresh lamb, let alone ripe mutton. One day, Bob Carpenter, a "hillbilly" from the Ozarks, claimed he could bring home a rabbit. Despite the sparse vegetation around the military base, there were a few wild rabbits, eking out an existence in the surrounding fields. Shooting at them was unthinkable, of course. But the radioman said he would use a homemade slingshot. Not only could he kill one, he bragged, but he could also hit one squarely in the head and leave the meat intact. Nobody believed him. Then he proved it, becoming quite popular as he hunted rabbits around the base and brought them to the camp cook to fry up a small feast for the crew.

The scarcity of meat made eggs a prized commodity. For British citizens, the weekly allowance was one fresh egg, plus a small portion of dried egg. U.S. Air Corps officers received two eggs per week.

"We treated them like gold," Pop said. "I kept these eggs in my locker till I wanted them for breakfast. Then I would take them to the cook at the mess hall, and he would cook them to order for me. That was a real treat and I looked forward to it each week."

Hearing about the rationing of eggs reminded me of my father's famous breakfasts of sautéed onions and eggs, gently scrambled in a pan full of melted butter. Although he was an excellent cook of all sorts of things—barbecued chicken, turkey stuffing, Dutch apple pie—it was his way of making scrambled eggs that was most memorable to me. It wasn't so much the actual dish that I loved but the attitude that went into making it. To the outside observer, it might seem to be a rather simple dish, but Pop was a perfectionist, making sure that every little detail was exactly right, taking great pride in preparing it just as he thought it should be. Every time I visited, I would awaken to the smell of coffee and the sound of my father pacing the floor, waiting for me to get up and get the day going.

"You gonna sleep till noon? What do you want for breakfast?" Pop would bark out, skipping the customary "Good morning." He always asked the same thing, and I always answered the same thing.

"Onions and eggs, please!"

In the later years, his failing vision required him to cook with just touch, smell, and intuition, and yet the dish always turned out perfectly.

The two comforts servicemen could count on were American cigarettes and cheap booze. Although food was in short supply, alcohol was plentiful in wartime England. But only gin and Scotch. And of course, my father was never much of a drinker. When on leave in London, he would occasionally come across a ration of beer, but it was always warm— "Yuck," declared Pop. Every two weeks the officers would take a train to London for a few days, but there wasn't much to do. Restaurants, when they could find one open, had little food, and practically no meat.

"Most of these poor people hadn't seen an egg for years," Pop marveled. "One of the restaurants I had dinner at featured Welsh Rabbit. I ordered it, thinking I would have meat, even if it were rabbit. To my surprise and disappointment, they served me cheese sauce on toast."

CHAPTER 7

Schiphol Airdrome

This job was not done without some loss to us, and before you get the impression that this was all a big picnic, I would like to give you as an example an account of the Amsterdam Schiphol mission on December 13, 1943....

...Of all the missions I have been on, that is the only one in which I felt sure I was going to get it. The flak was coming so thick and fast we were bouncing around like a canoe at sea. Shells were exploding all around us with mighty woffs and so many pieces of shell fragments were hitting us it felt as though a giant were throwing handfuls of rocks against the sides of the ship.

—Lieutenant Colonel Sherman R. Beaty

The altimeter on my personal Dreamliner Passenger Navigation video screen read -22 feet elevation as the aircraft lumbered through a maze of turns on the long taxi to the passenger gates at Schiphol Airport, Amsterdam. I peered out the window, imagining what I might have seen a couple hundred years ago: in a word, water. Once upon a time, the entire province of *Haarlemmermeer Polder*, where the airport lies, had been a large lake.

In the mid-eighteen hundreds, the lake was reclaimed, and Fort Schiphol was built. During World War I, a military airbase was constructed in 1916. *Haarlemmermeer* had once been a turbulent inland sea where many battles were fought, and many ships lost. Although the origin of the word *Schiphol* is debatable, many soldiers believe that it means "Ships' Hell" or "Ships' Grave." It's a good story, but no shipwrecks were ever found. Regardless of the meaning of the moniker, Schiphol played a critical role in both world wars, and today the North Holland airport is the busiest in Europe.

Lo and I were finally on our way to Belgium. Our trip had started with an exciting, yet exhausting international flight. We slept some, read some, watched a few movies. As the sun rose over the Celtic Sea, I awoke in my window seat, groggy but eager for the last thirty minutes of the flight. Studying our plane's course on the video screen, I was intrigued to see that our flight path was taking us right over northern England, across the Channel and into Schiphol. This course was eerily similar to the one my father had flown on what had been his most dangerous and terrifying mission, seventy-six years before.

As we approached the jetway, I kept thinking about this remarkable coincidence. After my father told me about bombing Schiphol Airdrome, I looked it up on *Wikipedia*: "An exceptionally heavy attack on 13 December 1943 caused so much damage that it rendered the airfield unusable as an active base." So, *this* was the airport that my father's group had bombed. Before planning our vacation, I had known virtually nothing about the city of Amsterdam, let alone anything about the airport. In 1940, the German military had captured the airport, renaming it *Fliegerhorst Schiphol* and installing anti-aircraft defenses. As a ruse to confuse Allied bombers like my father and his squadron, they built decoy airfields nearby; they even built a railway connection. Despite these defenses and deception, the airfield was ultimately bombed to smithereens. The Germans themselves finished the job when the Allies were poised to invade Germany.

Once inside the airport we followed the line of travel-stained passengers to the baggage claim, bracing ourselves for the long wait in customs and immigration. After a quick trip to the restroom, I fished my journal out of my travel bag to scrawl a note:

The Schiphol Airport restrooms have stalls that have walls from the floor up. No bottom gaps!

Whenever I travel, I keep a list of observations or feelings that pop into my head, quirky or profound, during my visit. Things that give a place perspective. By the end of our stay the list would contain such gems as:

I just don't get the waffle thing.

The concierge at our hotel pronounces the word gem like "gehm." We love it when he directs us to "hidden gehms" of Bruges.

Dutch and Belgians are warm and welcoming to Americans in spite of the fact that they dress better and have better manners than us.

While I was planning for the trip to Belgium, I visited my father in Arizona. It was lunchtime, and we were once again having our meal in the elegant dining room provided for the residents of Silver Springs.

"How's your soup?" I asked.

"Not hot enough."

I wasn't very hungry, and I wasted no time. Curious to hear the details of his Amsterdam mission, I asked him why the Allies were so intent on putting Schiphol out of commission.

"Schiphol Airdrome at Amsterdam was the largest and most important airdrome in Europe," he explained. "It had six runways, six to eight dispersal areas, and dozens of hangars and workshops. There were German bomber squadrons as well as fighters based there, and it was one of the main bases used to intercept our heavy bombers on their way to targets in Germany. Schiphol was so important that every B-26 available from our group and others in England were used to immobilize the base."

There was a reason the mission was to take so much firepower. The Germans depended on the anti-aircraft defenses of Schiphol airfield to keep the Allies out of Germany, and they were certain to defend it relentlessly. Major Sherman R. Beaty, the Commander of Pop's squadron that day, anticipated heavy and accurate flak on the bomb run, and in the target area. According to the intelligence briefing, approximately 128 flak guns surrounded the field.

This menacing flak was why my father called the squadron's bombing of Schiphol Airdrome his most dangerous mission.

✈ ✈
✈ ✈
✈ ✈

Flak: flyer defense cannons, from *Flugzeugabwehrkanone,* or *Flieger* (flyer) + *Abwehr* (defense) + *Kanonen* (cannons).

In 1944, flak accounted for 3,501 American planes destroyed, only 600 fewer than planes lost to enemy fighters in the same period. An incredible fifty-six bombers were destroyed or crippled by flak during a single B-17 raid on Merseburg in November of 1944.

Technically speaking, the cause of the Allied airmen's nightmares was the 8.8 cm flak 18/36/37/41—commonly called *flak* or the *eighty-eight.* If the B-26 was the bad-ass of the air, the 88 flak was the bad-ass on the ground. This aircraft-defense cannon was considered the second most effective weapon of World War II, after the atomic bomb. Deployed by the Germans to devastating effect, this flat-trajectory gun ruthlessly brought down thousands of bombers and tens of thousands of airmen.

Its design was devilishly clever. Flak artillery shells used fuses which were timed in their detonation. The shell would be launched from the artillery gun on the ground and, after a pre-set number of seconds, ignite the explosive compounds. To increase the devastation of the destruction, some shells were constructed with fragment shards—ball bearings or rails that were propelled by the blast of the warhead. Other types of shells were loaded with incendiary chemicals such as barium nitrate or phosphorous, creating a mid-air firestorm to effectively burn the bombers out of the sky.

Another piece to this diabolical weapon was called a "predictor," a device which could estimate where the targeted aircraft would be by the time the shell reached it, thus improving the shooter's aim and odds. The guns were grouped in fours, sharing one predictor. This allowed multiple guns to be aimed precisely at the same target by a single command crew of five men, instead of requiring trained crews on each gun. In daylight, the predictor crews used a telescope to follow the aircraft visually, while at night, sound locators directed the searchlights, which, in clear weather, had a range of about eight miles. The searchlights were sited in threes with a sound locator which, as its name implies, located the position of an aircraft by fixing on the sound of its engines.

The more important German targets—like Schiphol—were protected by up to forty heavy flak guns, firing rectangular patterns of shells known as "box barrages" that proved especially deadly. And since each battery was controlled by a single predictor, up to eighteen guns might engage one bomber at the same time. When the flak batteries pinpointed an aircraft, the guns were fired in salvos designed to burst in a sphere of sixty yards in diameter in which to entrap the target. Each gun could project a shell to 20,000 feet and could knock out an aircraft within thirty yards of the shell burst. The shrapnel from the explosion was capable of inflicting severe damage up to 200 yards.

I shuddered to imagine the stress, anxiety, and sheer terror of flying into flak, a regular occurrence for my father and his fellow airmen. It must have been a total assault on the senses, as well as the aircraft. The noise! Explosions so loud and frequent it must have been a constant drone, like the enraged alarm buzz of a threatened nest of hornets. And with the loudest of the explosions came the concussion, violently shaking the airplane as the pilots strained to focus and stay in tight formation though they could barely see anything. Every shell transformed into a cloud of black smoke, obscuring the sun above and the enemy below. I wondered aloud whether the thick, greasy smoke had a pungent odor.

"Hmm, I don't remember really smelling anything in the middle of all that," Pop commented dryly.

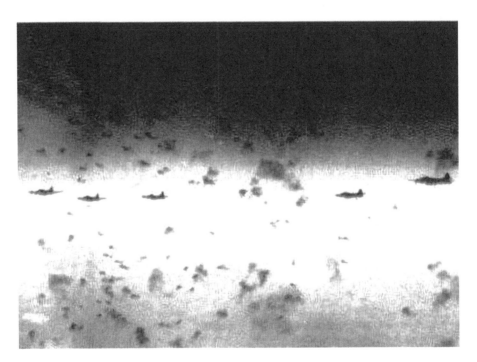

BOMBERS FLYING THROUGH A BARRAGE OF FLAK

"The B-26 was designed to destroy smaller targets by flying in tight formation at altitudes from nine to twelve thousand feet," my father told me. "This made us more vulnerable to anti-aircraft fire, but at this altitude, our bombing was much more accurate."

Low, accurate, and vulnerable or high, imprecise, and secure? This was the dilemma faced by commanders planning bombing raids over occupied Europe. Unlike her sister aircraft, the B-17, which bombed from twenty thousand feet or higher, the lower flying B-26 was much more accurate in hitting its targets, but the trade-off was the increased vulnerability to flak. As one young airman put it, "Holy shit! They are really shooting at us!" Just a slight deviation, even a few hundred feet, meant the difference between bombs destroying an airport, bridge, V-1 missile launch, or military factory, and a wasted mission risking many airmen's lives.

"Another reason accuracy was so important was that all our targets were in German-occupied France, Belgium, and Holland. Naturally, we wanted as few civilian casualties as possible," Pop explained. "When we reached our target for the day, if the target was not visible, we would return to our base, dropping the bombs in the North."

"Why did you drop them?" I asked.

"It was too dangerous to land with them still on board," he said.

So, throughout the war, the B-26 continued to fly right into the harrowing flak storms over their targets.

"Those in charge determined that, even though our losses would be high, the gains outweighed the losses," he concluded.

As if the stars had aligned with my renewed commitment to recording my father's stories, I happened upon *Martin B-26 Marauder, B-26.com*, a website created by Mike Smith for his great-uncle, Marauder Pilot Bob Brockett. Among the gallery of photos, diaries, and statistics was a detailed account of the Schiphol mission written by Chester P. Klier, historian for the 386th Bomb Group. Klier was aboard one of the planes during that mission, and his technical account, from Mission Briefing to touchdown, was harrowing.

Monday, December 13, 1943
386th Bomb Group
Mission Number 55

The afternoon briefing. Your target will be the Schiphol Airdrome, it is located four miles southwest of Amsterdam, Holland. Enemy flak batteries on the Dutch Coast will be able to fire at the formation, both going in and coming out. Heavy and accurate flak is to be expected on the bomb run, and in the target area.

This will be a multi group raid. The 323rd will lead, followed by the 387th, and 322nd Groups. Our 386th bunch will be the last formation to attack. Each group will supply eighteen planes plus two spares. Major Beaty will lead our effort, Captain Sands will head the high flight, with Captain Boyd White leading the low flight. All ships will carry four 1,000-pound general purpose demolition bombs.

You will rendezvous with the 322nd Group at 1407 hours over splasher beacon number seven. The 322nd will lead you to splasher beacon number six for a rendezvous with the 323rd formation, which will be accompanied by the 387th Bomb Group. The formation will proceed out over the North Sea to a point 52 degrees 10 minutes north, and 03 degrees 30 minutes east where you will rendezvous with your Spitfire fighter escort at 1445 hours. Two to three squadrons of Spitfires will make strafing sweeps of the target area ahead of the bomber attack, with the hope the Jerries will be pinned down when you make your bomb run.

You will encounter cloud build up near the English Coast and extending to mid-point over the North Sea with a base of 2,000 feet and tops to 4,000 feet. Visibility will be ten miles with patches of stratocumulus at 2,000 feet along the coast of Holland. The target will have ceiling unlimited, visibility six miles or better with a chance of light haze.

Flight crews left the briefing room at 1220 hours; within five minutes they arrived at their assigned aircraft. The Group started engines at 1255 hours.

As my father reclined in his old easy chair, re-living the experience, eyes closed, he recalled the first mishap of the mission: "I was flying a plane named 'MISS MURIEL.' Our group of eighteen planes arrived at the rendezvous point over the North Sea right on time...." He paused.

"But no one was there!"

So much for the best laid plans.

According to the Mission Plan, the four bomber groups were supposed to rendezvous over the English Channel, then proceed to the target as one formation. This was not a simple sequence to execute, especially since military aircraft had to forgo radio contact as it would tip off the enemy. Unable to communicate, the airmen relied on basic navigation, timing, visuals, and blind luck. As detailed in the mission briefing that morning, my father's 386th was to be the last of the groups to arrive over "splasher beacon number seven." The Squadron Commander, Major Beaty, and his group arrived at the appointed time only to find empty air space.

Determined to execute the mission as planned, Major Beaty set a course for the next navigation beacon as every eye in the lonely squadron scanned the sky for the missing mother formation. After an agonizing few minutes, Major Beaty spotted the bomber group far ahead, and he cut toward it. He pushed his aircraft to a dizzying 205 miles per hour, desperate to catch up, but he could not close the gap. Inexplicably, the others had left the rendezvous point a full two minutes ahead of schedule.

This was not good. *Really* not good.

"This put us, the last ones over the target, *all by ourselves!*" Pop said, recalling his horror at the realization.

Bombers fly in formation for reasons both offensive and defensive.

"Formation bombing was the method we used," he continued. "This type of bombing relied on all the planes in the formation to drop their bombs at the same time, forming a pattern on the target. To accomplish this, the bombardier in each plane kept an eye on the lead plane: When the lead plane opened his bomb bay doors, each bombardier opened his, and when the first bomb was released, each plane would do the same."

Formation bombing also has a defensive element. The tight formation presents a smaller target for both enemy fighters and flak; plus, it creates a higher concentration of gunner defense around the planes. These small advantages are critical. But now, because they were separated from the mother formation, my father's group would be late to the party, and the party was an enraged hornet's nest of determined Germans waiting to blow them out of the sky.

"The Germans knew we were coming, and defense of the airdrome was imperative, so the flak would be merciless," Pop told me.

"This is probably a silly question," I interrupted. "But how did the Germans know you were coming?"

"We flew only daylight missions, hitting specific targets—factories, bridges, munitions dumps, and so on," he explained. "So, regardless of the precautions we took, such as not using our radios, we were flying over enemy-occupied France and Belgium to get to Amsterdam. Soldiers on the ground and enemy planes in the air would see us and report, giving them at least a little time to predict where we were headed and start preparing."

"I see," I nodded.

The German soldiers manning the anti-aircraft guns on the ground needed time to precisely calculate how to hit the target nine to twelve thousand feet above them, based on speed, altitude, and wind. This tricky process would be largely dialed in once the mother squadron had passed. My father's group, minutes behind, would be right in their crosshairs. And there was no way for Pop and the 386th to deviate from the flight plan as the planes were bound by the demands of the B-26's Norden bombsight, the piece of equipment that was used to direct the bomber over the target and indicate when to release the bombs. At the time, the Norden was the most sophisticated and accurate device of its kind, and its technology was closely guarded. Bombardiers were required to take an oath stating that they would defend the Norden with their own lives. If an aircraft should make an emergency landing on enemy territory, the bombardier's first duty was to shoot the bombsight with a gun to disable it. After each completed mission, the precious cargo was immediately removed from the aircraft to be deposited in a safe called "The Bomb Vault."

But the accuracy of the Norden came at a cost.

"The Norden had to be programmed with the airspeed, altitude, and direction the plane was flying," Pop told me. "The crosshairs in the bombsight had to be locked on the target for one full minute. This meant that during the final portion of the run, we had to maintain the programmed information exactly, flying in a straight line toward the target. We could not take any evasive action even if we were attacked by fighters, or if the anti-aircraft shells were bursting all around us."

So, on the way to the target, the pilots could maneuver the planes trying to evade both fighters and flak. But then, as they approached the target, the bombsight required pilots to fly completely uniform in speed, elevation, and direction, for a full minute, becoming targets themselves for flak. In those final critical moments before dropping the bomb load onto the small target far below, they had to fly in a straight line—lined up like ducks for the hunter.

"It wasn't a matter of *if* we would be hit," Pop continued. "It was *how bad.*"

I half-jokingly remarked that if I were piloting that plane under those conditions I would have turned around and got the hell out of there.

"You never, *ever* leave the formation unless you're going down," Pop informed me sternly.

Klier's account continues:

Major Beaty's formation reached the I. P. and took up a heading of 285 degrees; a huge gap of some four or five miles existed between him and the other groups ahead. His Bombardier Lieutenant William Leirevaag called for a five-degree correction to the left, and the 280-degree bomb run was underway as he hunched over his Norden Bomb Sight! The 88mm flak was all about them, very intense and extremely accurate. It could be heard exploding nearby—Shoomp, Whooph, Whooph! Bomb bay doors were open, air speed 190 m.p.h. Captain Sanford pulled "HELL'S FURY" up close behind his leader so close he was looking straight up at Beaty's tail gunner. Both of Sandford's wingmen moved in closer. Lieutenant Albert Burger flying "YANKEE DOODLE DANDY" 131947 YA-D on right and Lieutenant Roy Voorhees flying "LADY FROM HADES" 131685 YA-J on the left. An unusual number of large persistent pink bursts preceded a heavy concentration of both white and black bursts. A piece of flak sheared off the pitot tube on "STAR DUST" 134937 YA-N in number two position of the low flight flown by Lieutenant R.D. Wilson.

Number four ship was hit—as noted by number six man Lieutenant Voorhees. Captain Sanford's airplane sustained a direct hit which appeared to be on the left main fuel tank, the plane burst into flames immediately! Lieutenant Burger, number five man stated, Sanford's ship had a direct hit on a wing, and lost wing when it folded over fuselage and burning. The heat from the burning plane was so intense the controls and paint on his wing men's ships were warped and blistered and even the gunners felt the heat on their backs. It went straight down and exploded. Staff Sergeant E.O. Stensrud was tail gunner on the lead ship and looking down on the Sanford plane. He related—direct hit, the plane nosed up and the left engine burst into flame. Then it nosed down with a half twist to the left, and headed straight to the deck!

The stricken aircraft made a Split-S and was on a reciprocal heading when aerial photographer Tech Sergeant Edward H. Lynch caught sight of it. He was flying in a plane named "MISS MURIEL" 131796 YA-H piloted by Flight Officer Wasowicz. They were in number six position of the low flight. With one wing off, "HELL'S FURY" rolled over on its back just as the photographer got off a shot. He cocked the shutter and fired off another shot as the ship tucked its nose under and went into a dive!

"I just remember seeing the smoke from miles ahead," Pop said. "We were still several minutes behind the rest of the planes, and by the time we got there, it was a thick, black cloud—so thick I could barely see. There was an explosion, and a plane went down. The group photographer, riding in my plane for this mission, caught a picture of that plane the moment it exploded about fifty feet below us. Let me tell you, I was never that scared in my life!"

HELL'S FURY EXPLODING MIDAIR

My father's account of the bomb run was vivid, as if it had happened just last week. He spoke slowly and seemed to relive the terror of the flak: "All the anti-aircraft fire was concentrated on us. The shells exploded all around us."

After dropping the bombs, the severely hobbled squadron turned and raced away with 125 miles of open sea still between them and England. Their nerves must have been as rattled as much as their aircrafts. Back at their home base, the emotionally battered crews reported for mission interrogation.

"We only lost one plane out of our eighteen, but after landing at our home base, we learned that every plane had at least four major holes," Pop told me.

Of the eighteen planes from my father's group that took off that day, there were five single engine landings and two crash landings; the remaining eleven planes were out of commission for a full week due to flak damage. There were ten men wounded, several critically, and six missing in action—the crew of HELL'S FURY, piloted by Captain Ray Sanford. Many of the crews reported seeing Sanford's plane go down; all aboard were presumed dead.

Still, the mission was a success, especially considering the ferocity of the flak. Major Beaty later declared, "I honestly believe no other plane could have come through such a barrage of fire with such a low loss ratio as those Marauders. Personally, I owe the lives of my crew and myself to the ability of the B-26 to take such terrific punishment and still keep flying."

"That B-26 saved my life, and the lives of my crew," Pop agreed.

While the aircraft were being repaired, the flight crews were given four-day passes.

"This gave us an opportunity to visit London, see the damage done by the Germans' V-2 rockets, and relax a little."

"What did you do to relax?" I asked him.

"Oh, there wasn't too much relaxing due to air raids, running to bomb shelters, very little food in the restaurants, and a shortage of everything except beer and gin," he said wearily. It was getting close to suppertime, and Pop looked exhausted, so we decided to take a break.

✈ ✈
✈ ✈
✈ ✈

We had a light supper, and then my father had a little more to say about his most dangerous mission.

"After our so-called R and R in London, when we returned to our base, we were surprised to see everyone digging foxholes," he began. "Apparently, the day before, a German fighter plane strafed the field. Maybe they didn't like what we did to their airbase in Holland."

The demanding Schiphol mission was an important Allied victory. It seems odd to think of it that way, but that is what it says in the history books—*an exceptionally heavy attack on 13 December 1943 caused so much damage that it rendered the airfield unusable as an active base.*

During my conversations with my father, I was often on the edge of my seat, nodding eagerly and taking notes, but Pop usually spoke evenly, with little drama. He told me that he was concerned that his stories might seem too exciting or heroic. To him, they were neither. After sowing his wild oats during his flight training, he became profoundly aware that, as a bomber pilot, he was responsible for the lives of others as well as his own. And there were plenty of military casualties. Recounting the Amsterdam mission, my father told me that, on just that one bomb run to Schiphol, more than one hundred officers were killed, including the Base Commander. This was something Pop could never be proud of.

"But still," I argued. "You must have been at least a little bit proud that you helped to destroy the enemy airfield."

He paused before answering.

"Of course, we felt pretty good about the job we did, in spite of all that flak," Pop told me. But as I told you, we flew only daylight missions, hitting specific targets: factories, bridges, munitions dumps, and so on. But the British heavy bombers carried twice the load of bombs that our planes could and flew only at night, at very high altitude. Their method of bombing was called *area bombing*. One plane at a time would fly over a city and drop its load of bombs. There was no precision because they didn't need precision. After my release from prison camp, I had a chance to see the results of this type of bombing as I flew over some of the devastation. I did not see a single roof on any of the homes in some of those cities."

He sat back, tired.

"It was horrible," he said grimly. "I was glad I didn't have to be involved in that."

Following the crushing success of the Schiphol mission, the former airbase served only as an emergency landing field until, under retreat, the Germans themselves destroyed its remnants.

After the war, Schiphol Airdrome was promptly rebuilt, and it has become one of the world's busiest international airports. But once a year, at eight in the evening, there is silence at Schiphol. No planes may land, taxi, or even start their engines. The music in shops and restaurants is turned off. For two minutes on this annual day for Remembrance of the Dead, all Dutch pause to commemorate the civilians and soldiers who have made the ultimate sacrifice since the beginning of World War II. This day of commemoration happens every May 4th.

CHAPTER 8

Mission 18

Captain called for a watch synchronization; ten second count down. The airmen dramatically emptied their pockets of personal items, wallets, photos, and the like into a bag to be retrieved after they return. In exchange they were handed escape kits containing high energy food, a dime size compass, and a cloth map of the Continent. Also a packet of escape money as they filed out of the briefing room.

Air Battle summary: Altitude was 12,000 feet, the formation was flying 190 m.p.h. Our gunners shot down a FW-190 and a Me-109. We lost one bomber.

—Chester P. Klier, Historian, 386th Bomb Group

I kept an eye on my father's mood and stamina, trying not to agitate or overtire him. Most of the time, he seemed ready to tell me anything I asked, anything he could remember, that is. After recounting the long story of the Schiphol mission, we had called it a night. The next day, rested, he seemed eager to get back to it.

"Anyway, my crew ended up with a total of seventeen missions," he informed me.

"Seventeen missions?" I asked, confused. "I thought you had flown *eighteen* missions."

"Seventeen *successful* missions," Pop stated coldly.

On January 23, 1944, the day of his eighteenth mission, my father's crew had been a last-minute addition to a bombing raid over occupied France. Pop and his men had not originally been among those assigned to pilot this mission but, fatefully, one of the pilots woke up with a bad cold that day, so my father and his crew were called in to replace them. Trained as a team, they flew as a team. If any member of a bomber crew was not able to fly, the entire crew was grounded, a rule that was strictly enforced.

"It really was a very good system," Pop assured me. "I knew exactly what to expect from each man, and they knew what to expect from me."

Following the morning mission briefing, my father and his crew hurried across the rainy, windy tarmac to their assigned aircraft—a B-26 named "EXTERMINATOR." Pop's first recollection of the day was of his baseball cap—the one he had worn all through training and on every single one of his seventeen successful missions. As he jogged to the airplane, the wind blew his cap off his head. He chased it down and plucked it out of a mud puddle.

"This was my good luck cap, the one I never flew without. I knew then that this was going to be a bad day!" he said, shaking his head.

A few minutes later, in a hurry to start the pre-flight check, he hastily stuffed the dirty wet cap behind his seat.

✈ ✈
✈ ✈
✈ ✈

Our last night in Amsterdam, I wrote a postcard to my father:

Hi Pop! Lo & I are having a blast in Amsterdam. Amazing city—the canals are beautiful and it's surprisingly quiet and clean. You would love the food. We're eating tons of all the classics—haring, mussels, and frites (French fries). Not crazy about the waffles, but the coffee shops are great! Nothing like Starbucks! Plenty of culture and history, too. Went to the Rijksmuseum and saw the Old Masters, also the Van Gogh Museum (my favorite) and heard some Beethoven at the symphony hall. Off to Bruges tomorrow. Wish you were here! Love, Tony & Lo

P.S., Schiphol Airport forgives you.

While focusing mainly on our trip to Belgium, I had still wanted to maximize our brief time in Amsterdam. On one very full day, Lo and I not only toured the Van Gogh Museum, but also went to a concert at the Royal *Concertgebouw*. The grand building had been inspired by the second *Gewandhaus* in Leipzig. Another casualty of World War II, that *Gewandhaus* had been destroyed during the fire bombings in 1943. The *Concertgebouw* escaped devastation during the war, and although it has been extensively renovated since its grand opening in 1888, superstitious Dutch believe that removing the layer of dust in the Main Hall would alter its famous acoustics. As on that April day in 1888, Beethoven was the headliner, along with Rachmaninoff. It was ironic to note that, during World War II, the Nazis had co-opted Beethoven's music for their propaganda purposes, and as a result, his music was banned in some Allied countries.

We had excellent seats, high in the mezzanine, and during the performance, I noticed an elderly gentleman, accompanied by a younger man, whom I supposed must be his son. Having my own father on my mind, I found myself stealing glances at them. I observed the way the old man was dressed—crisp dress shirt, tie, jacket. I knew somehow that it had not been his son or anyone else who had dressed him. He must have insisted on doing it himself, I thought, and doing it well, too. Why? Because he was at the end of his life, time was running out. And he knew it. But why should he care about what he was wearing? Why not take it easy, go for comfort? No one would hold it against him. I admired his dignity, his apparent determination to go on being the person he had always been as long as he lived. The son kept looking over at him anxiously. The old man, head nodding, fell fast asleep about ten minutes into Beethoven's Pastoral Symphony.

For dinner on our last evening in Amsterdam, we found a *rijsttafel*, Dutch for "rice table." *Rijsttafel* involves an elaborate meal of Indonesian dishes developed during the Dutch colonial era. In another little coincidence, we noted that we had visited Sumatra twenty-five years ago, that we had eaten the original Indonesian version of *rijsttafel*, and that we happened to be there on the day Indonesians celebrate their independence from the Netherlands. Dutch rule ended during World War II when the Japanese invaded and occupied the archipelago.

We loved Amsterdam, and there was still plenty of rich history, culture, and food to experience, but it was time to move on. The wonders of Bruges awaited. Inspired by the film *In Bruges*, we were impatient to see this unspoiled medieval city for ourselves.

We spent our last evening in Amsterdam doing our own version of a mission briefing. After re-packing our suitcases, we reviewed our tickets, maps, and reservations. The plan was simple—quick cab ride to the Amsterdam train station; nice continental breakfast; comfy-class train ride; get off at Antwerp and wander the city for a couple of hours; then hop on the train to Bruges; quick cab to the Van Cleef, our canal-side hotel. Let the fairytale vacation begin.

We arrived in Antwerp, and all was going according to plan: Our luggage stowed in a locker, we began by admiring the architecture of the glorious "railroad cathedral," or Antwerp Central Railway Station, a restored version of the one that was bombed during World War II. Belgium is known as the "Battlefield of Europe," and, unlike the miraculous protection that the city of Bruges had enjoyed, the recent history of Antwerp was no fairytale. Emerging from the elegant train station, Rick Steves's guidebook in hand, we encountered a modern city, apparently still rebuilding seventy years after the end of the war. In the midst of the contemporary buildings, the 16th Century City Hall and the 19th Century Brabo Fountain were reminders of the prewar city. But today Antwerp is a trendy destination, renowned for its fashion industry and diamond trade—in fact, the vast majority of all diamonds are traded there. What we didn't know was that during World War II, Antwerp was a principal target of Hitler's secret weapon.

It all started in Holland. Looking to take over Rotterdam, the largest seaport in Europe, Hitler's army invaded the Netherlands in 1940. When the Germans met resistance, the *Luftwaffe* relentlessly bombed Rotterdam, destroying its city center. Next on Hitler's wish list was Antwerp. Joined to the North Sea by the River Scheldt, Antwerp is the *second* largest port in Europe. Unlike Rotterdam's Dutch resistance, Antwerp followed Belgian neutrality, a policy which left the whole country vulnerable and defenseless, and once Rotterdam fell to the Nazis, Antwerp quickly succumbed. Suddenly, the German government, administration, and police forces had their iron grip on the port city. The merciless invasion intensified persecution of Jews, exacerbated food shortages, and expanded forced labor.

One by one, the Nazis robbed the people of their individual freedoms. All Antwerpians were repressed, but especially members of the large Jewish community, many of them refugees who had fled persecution in their native countries. The Nazis banned ritual slaughter; they excluded Jews from certain professions; they forced Jews aged fifteen and older to register with the German administration. This persecution went on and on. In 1941, all Jewish identification cards were stamped with the brand *Jood-Juif*, and Jewish children were banned from public institutions. Whenever they were in public, all Jews aged six years and older were forced to wear a yellow Star of David on their clothing. The administration distributed approximately 15,000 of these badges in Antwerp, and they kept precise records of residents who refused to wear them.

The years dragged on. The already dire food shortages known to all Europeans became desperate as food was rigorously rationed and regulated. A meaningless coupon system was implemented; an empty piece of symbolism, a coupon could not pay for food but merely signified that the holder was entitled to a specific product, products that were mostly nowhere to be found.

And then they were enslaved. Beginning in 1940, nearly 3,000 Antwerp Jews and other foreigners were rounded up and taken to forced labor camps around Belgium. By the summer of 1942, forced labor was expanded to German military building projects in northern France and, after that, inside Germany itself. More than 10,000 Jews were deported from Antwerp that year. If the forced labor camps were horrific, the death camps were hell itself. At the end of October, the labor camps were evacuated, and an estimated eighty percent of the prisoners ended their days in Auschwitz.

The brutal German occupation lasted more than four long years. But on June 6, 1944—D-Day—the tide of World War II finally turned. In September, British tanks rumbled through the streets of Antwerp, lined with cheering Belgians. By the end of November, the first Allied ship sailed into the port. The liberation had begun, but the war was far from over. Although German soldiers were on the run, they still held positions in the city, and the fighting continued. In some ways, the worst was yet to come. A vengeful Hitler, unwilling to leave the prized port city to his enemies, unleashed the very latest in German warfare technology—his secret weapon.

Developed in 1936, the V-2 Rocket —*Vergeltungswaffen-2*, or Vengeance Weapon-2—was the world's first ballistic, supersonic missile. Flying at over four times the speed of sound, it could not be tracked by radar, brought down by Allied aircraft or artillery fire, or even *seen* in time to sound an air raid siren. At that time, there was no defense against these unstoppable missiles. It was these German V-2 launching sites that were targeted by my father's squadron during his eighteenth mission in January 1944.

When the Allies began bombing German cities, the Germans used this "vengeance weapon" to punish Allied cities. In a fit of retaliative rage, Hitler launched thousands of these V-2 missiles upon the city of Antwerp, a six-month assault that was also a last-ditch effort to hold on to some of the ground he had held for four years. Demonstrating just how desperate he was, the leader of the Third Reich launched more V-2 rockets on Antwerp than on all other targets attacked during the entire war, *combined.* Casualties were estimated at 3,000 civilians and 600 Allied troops killed during the assault.

The V-2, however, had one major flaw: inaccuracy. In the end, the ferocious assault failed to destroy the all-important port. On March 28, the last flying bomb landed in Greater-Antwerp. The besieged city was in ruins, but it was finally free.

Now, seventy-four years later, Lo and I found ourselves ambling around Antwerp, the diamond capital of the world. Without yet knowing the tumultuous history of Antwerp, we strolled the *Grote Markt* in the heart of the old city quarter. We window-shopped in an opulent mall, full of couture shops and chic cafés. An atmosphere of vibrancy filled the streets teeming with tourists and locals alike, all clutching smartphones, designer purses, and shopping bags. It had taken decades to recover, rebuild, and restore a sense of normalcy. A Ten-Year Plan had been devised in 1956 to modernize the port's infrastructure, attract new industry, and revitalize the economy. Improvements continued even as we admired the glossy new buildings.

For lunch, we were a little surprised to find some first-rate sushi in a Japanese restaurant near the Cathedral of Our Lady. In front of the cathedral we happened upon a marble statue of a boy and his dog covered by a cobblestone blanket, a touching monument to *A Dog of Flanders*, the 1872 story by the English novelist known as Ouida. In the 1980s, Antwerp city guides had begun noticing Japanese tourists weeping outside the cathedral, the site where the boy Nello and his dog Patrasche are found frozen to death in the final scene of the novel. Wildly popular in Japan for decades, the Flemish fairytale has been adapted into several Japanese films and *anime;*

Japanese automaker Toyota had even donated a commemorative plaque. Today, we were seeing a modern marble sculpture created by Belgian artist Batist Vermeulen in 2016. Even we, with our limited knowledge of history, marveled at this contemporary tableau in which the cultures of former mortal enemies had become entwined. While Hitler was rampaging through Europe, Hirohito had been doing his worst in the Pacific. Decades after the Allied Powers defeated the Axis, the Allied city of Antwerp welcomed the people of formerly Axis Japan with sushi restaurants and a marble tribute to Flemish storybook characters that have become beloved Japanese icons.

Meandering back to the Antwerp station, aglow after a long, relaxing lunch, we were getting excited to finally be going to Bruges. We got our luggage out of the locker, and I looked for our train on the big board. No train to Bruges. I looked some more. I'd had a large Sapporo beer at lunch and thought I might be a little muddled. I looked more carefully. Still no train to Bruges. A bit of panic came over me—things like this never go well. As both pilot and navigator of this mission, I stationed Lo next to the luggage, found a line that seemed to lead to an official looking man, and stood in it. After a long, anxious wait, I stepped up to the window ready to ask about the train to Bruges, but the clerk anticipated me, whispering solemnly, "There's been an *accident*!—a *fire*! There is no train to Bruges."

We plan, God laughs.

I nodded with a mirthless chuckle. Not about the accident and fire, of course, just at the perversity of the universe. But the clerk's face brightened, and he scribbled some names on a scrap of paper.

"Take this train to Brussels," he said confidently, "and connect with this train to Bruges."

Yes—all was well again!

All was well, that is, until we missed the stop in Brussels because we don't speak French, and we misread the signs, and so we sat with our hands in our laps as the train left the city and barreled toward France. It took an hour, but with the help of a kind and understanding conductor, we were able to get off, turn around, and then finally get on board a train to Bruges. The ride through the Belgian countryside was as beautiful as it was long. Along the way, the train stopped briefly at Waterloo, which reminded us once again how little we remembered our European history and geography. Napoleon's French army had been defeated. Tens of thousands of soldiers were killed. And for what? What was it all about? We decided we needed to study up on that historic battle and return to Waterloo someday, walking in the footsteps of Napoleon.

The train crawled along, like a city bus stopping at every corner, dropping off locals. I fixated on the fact that we were losing precious hours, hours that we should have been spending relaxing in Bruges. Lo could see I was upset. I had carried our heavy bags up and down several stairways at the bustling Brussels station, trying to decipher the signs and find the right platform, and I was sweating with exhaustion and worry.

"It's not your fault," she said. "It's still early, and we're finally on the right track."

"Funny," I said glumly as she poked my ribs. Then the train slowed, and I looked out at the signs again. The train had arrived at the small station in Ghent, yet another lucky city that somehow escaped massive destruction, despite being occupied by the Germans during both World Wars.

"Hey, this is the last stop before Bruges," I informed Lo. "We're getting close!" And then it struck me—this little hamlet was near Gravelines, the very spot where my father's airplane was shot down in 1944. Shaking off my self-pity, I perked up again, craning my neck to see out the window. It would be nice to get a picture for Pop, but there wasn't much to see aside from the concrete platform of the train station. And, with my luck, just like in the movies, I'd wander off a bit too far: The train doors slam shut, Lo's horrified eyes stare frantically through the window as the train disappears into the mist to Bruges, without me.

Instead, I gazed up into what bit of the sky I could see and tried to imagine what a group of Allied bombers would look like flying twelve thousand feet above me. I visualized a chaotic, vicious firefight mid-air, and a B-26 engulfed in flames.

On the fateful day in 1944, my father told me, the mission had been straightforward.

"The targets for that day were German rocket launch sites near the French coast," Pop began. "These launch sites were used to send rocket-propelled robot planes, called V-2 Rockets, or Buzz Bombs, filled with explosives. Launched across the Channel, the rocket propellant was timed to expire over the city of London where the weapon would plummet and explode in the streets."

A squadron of eighteen Martin B-26 Marauders would cross the English Channel into enemy-occupied France, turn north along the coast, and bomb the German V-2 rocket launching sites that were terrorizing civilians throughout London.

"The position in the formation I was assigned to was nicknamed 'coffin corner,'" Pop continued ominously. More bad luck after the windblown and muddied ballcap.

"I'm afraid to ask," I said.

"It was called *coffin corner* because it was the easiest plane for fighters to hit by coming in from the rear, picking off the corner plane of the formation, and then swinging off, in this case to the right, and thus minimizing the machine gun fire from the rest of the formation."

Unlike the Schiphol mission, this time, the bomb run itself had gone relatively smoothly. So far, so good.

"There were several small targets," Pop explained, "so once we were over the coast of France, we split the formation into three six-plane units and headed on our separate runs. We dropped our bombs successfully on our assigned targets, re-formed our eighteen-plane formation, and headed home."

They were lucky that day—at first. During the bomb run, thirteen of the planes had been hit by ground flak fire, but no significant damage was done. Then, three minutes after bombs-away, a flight of four enemy Focke-Wulf-190 fighter planes broke through the bomber cover near the city of Ghent and attacked the formation. They made straight for EXTERMINATOR in the coffin corner of the formation.

My father described the attack: "As we approached the French coast, an FW-190 German fighter plane dropped out of a cloud, right on my tail. He peppered my plane with 20mm armor piercing and explosive shells, setting the radio compartment, bomb bay, and the left engine on fire."

It was another hard twist of fate. Had it been another type of enemy aircraft, the outcome might have been different. But the Focke-Wulf-190 happened to be the only fighter in the sky that was equipped with a 20mm-nose cannon, which spits out shells instead of bullets. These massive shells came in two deadly designs that were fired in sequence—the solid armor-piercing shells would penetrate the exterior of an aircraft, allowing the lighter, explosive-filled shells to wreak havoc on the interior. Worse, I learned later, the lead pilot of the Focke-Wulf pack was an ace, with a wartime total of twenty-one kills to his credit. Swooping in behind my father's plane, the German ace released a violent flurry of cannon shells, spraying the entire B-26. Cannon shells penetrated the navigation compartment, directly behind the pilot's seat, and then exploded. Flames erupted inside the aircraft.

"I was hit in the neck and my right hand, which was on the throttles," Pop began. "The cockpit filled with smoke, and I couldn't see anything through the windshield. I had a difficult time controlling the plane, so my main concern was to get out of formation."

You never, ever leave the formation unless you're going down, I grimly recalled Pop telling me earlier.

"I *had* to drop out of the formation to avoid hitting one of the other planes in formation. I pulled back on the throttles, but I couldn't see through the smoke, so I opened the side window and stuck my head out to check my position. A few seconds later, the right side-engine went out. The aircraft was going down."

Pop took a deep breath before continuing.

"The fire was burning out of control, so I hit the bailout bell, which was supposed to sound throughout the plane, to order the crew to bail out. But I couldn't be sure the guys in back would get the message with all the wiring on fire."

"I think I would have hit the panic button," I joked, imagining my state of mind inside the cockpit of a burning B-26, with my hand and neck bleeding.

"No, you wouldn't," Pop insisted. "You'd have had the same training I had. We practiced over and over and over—every procedure was drilled into our brains. We didn't even really need to think, not that there was time. Anyway, my next problem was to keep control of the plane as long as possible, allowing enough time for the crew to bail out."

While fighting to keep the doomed bomber flying straight and level on just one engine, my father turned his attention to his Navigator, Lieutenant Gemery, who had been stationed in the nose cone of the plane behind a .50 Browning machine gun.

"Why was the navigator behind the gun in the nose?" I interrupted, recalling my anxiety attack inside the B-26 nose cone.

"Remember, I told you that in any given formation of bombers, it's only the lead aircraft that does the navigating and initial release of the bombs. The rest of the pack follows his neighbor, turning when she does and dropping the bombs when she does. After dropping the bombs, Gemery was stationed where he should have been, where he could be most useful."

As for poor Gemery, if the ordeal of having to squat in the nose of a bomber while being attacked from above and below wasn't enough, the narrow opening to the nose cone precluded the navigator's wearing of a bulky parachute. His chute, the only means of making it out alive, was stashed in the burning navigation compartment. As my father continued to struggle with the controls, he yelled to his co-pilot, F/O McClanahan, to get back there and grab Gemery's parachute. McClanahan dove into the burning compartment but emerged seconds later empty handed, saying that there was just too much fire back there. Pop recalled turning, looking into his eyes, and firmly saying, "We need that chute!"

McClanahan immediately dove back into the flames, eventually emerging with severe burns all over his arms, neck, and back. He had also taken a hit of shrapnel in the back. He handed Gemery the parachute.

"The next problem we encountered was the hydraulic system, which was partially damaged," Pop explained. "The only exit from the forward section of the plane was through the nose wheel compartment, the open bomb bay, or the side windows in the rear of the plane. Since access to the rear was blocked by fire, our only hope was the nose wheel compartment."

Pop hit the lever to drop the wheel and make space to evacuate, but nothing happened.

McClanahan reported that there was just enough hydraulic pressure to open the compartment doors, but not enough to drop the nose wheel.

"I told Mac, a robust Indiana farm boy, to try jumping up and down on the wheel and hopefully force it down," Pop went on. "This tactic worked, and the wheel was forced down far enough for a man to sit on the wheel and slide out."

My father held on to the controls while Gemery sat on the wheel and slid out, but McClanahan hesitated

"He didn't want to leave me in a burning airplane that was probably going to explode," Pop said. "But I told him I was right behind him."

McClanahan reluctantly squeezed through the gap.

With the Co-pilot and Navigator out of the doomed bomber, it was the Pilot's turn to bail out. Instead, he stayed in his pilot's seat, head out the window, gripping the controls of the disintegrating aircraft.

"Why didn't you bail out then?" I asked.

"I didn't have any way of knowing when, or if, the three crewmen in the rear of the plane bailed out because the entire bomb bay and the radio compartment were engulfed in flames," Pop explained.

Fully expecting the bomber to explode in mid-air, my father was going to sacrifice his own life to increase the chances of the others.

"I just sat there, keeping control of the plane for as long as I could to give the men in the rear a chance to get out."

As if in a trance, he kept the bomber in the air, waiting for the onboard ammunition to explode.

"This ammunition ran on belts along the inside of the fuselage and was used in the four .50 caliber machine guns under my control," Pop explained. "After what seemed to be a long time, but probably only a few minutes, I heard the ammunition for our machine guns exploding from the heat."

The explosion awakened my father as from a dream. In a sudden moment of clarity, a single, absolute thought popped into his head: *It's time to get out, now!*

"The plane had not blown up as I expected, so I thought that maybe I had a chance to get out. I released the control wheel, got out of my seat, hurriedly sat on top of the exposed nose wheel, and slid out!"

"Holy smokes!" I said.

"I was happy to get out," he said simply.

"Holy smokes!" I said again.

Now, sitting in his old recliner in the dim light of his memory, he told me that, despite the continuous explosion of flak around him, it had been strangely quiet and peaceful, sitting there in the pilot seat, waiting for the moment, the end.

Drained for the day, we said our goodnights and went to bed. I dreamed I was back in Florida at the Fantasy of Flight Air Museum, trapped in the nose cone of the Martin B-26 Marauder. Claustrophobic and scared, I tried to divert my thoughts—*serenity now, serenity now, serenity now....* But attempts at calming myself were besieged by thoughts of Lieutenant Gemery, the Navigator/Bombardier of Pop's crew, and the story Pop had told me about that fateful mission. Horrific images flashed through my mind. And, over the pounding of the mortar rounds and the white noise of the peppering flak, there was an explosion behind me. The blast was intense, and the concussion was further amplified within the tiny nose cone. In an instant the airplane was on fire and going down. And I was trapped in a bubble barely big enough to sit in and I had no parachute....

CHAPTER 9

Interrogation

As EXTERMINATOR nosed out of formation under control, three chutes emerged, and landing gear was lowered. The bomber entered a cloud, and one chute plummeted out of the nose wheel doors. EXTERMINATOR crashed one and a half miles west of Fort Phillipe, NNW of Loom Plage 3 miles east of Gravelines, France.

Crew: F/O.s Barney W. Wasowicz; Harold R McClanahan; 2.Lt Matthew Gemery; S/Sqts Robert D Carpenter; Lewis G Fischer; Lester D Higgins.

—Trevor Allen, Historian, B-26.com

In the morning, my father and I went to breakfast in the dining room.

"How's the coffee?" I asked. "And your eggs?"

"Not bad," he said. "I told you before, everything here is very good. Just not hot enough."

I wanted to know what had happened to Pop when he bailed out of his B-26, so after breakfast, we settled back into his apartment. Never having parachuted out of an airplane myself, I asked him what it was like to fall out of the sky.

"Were you scared?"

"No, not really. Like I said, I was happy to get out of there," he began. "When you have shells bursting all around you and a hot fire on your rear end, believe me, you would be happy to get out!"

I had to laugh. Only my Pop would say "rear end."

"I pulled the ripcord and the parachute opened," he went on. "I had this wonderful feeling of just hanging in the sky, in perfect silence. A giant hook in the sky was holding me up there; there wasn't a sound to be heard. I had no sensation of falling, and I sat there in my parachute harness, just enjoying the sensation. Until the last hundred feet. When I looked down, I saw the earth rushing up to meet me. Took me by surprise. I couldn't figure out how to turn around and face forward—I never had any parachute training."

"Wait, what? Why not?" I asked, taken aback.

"Who knows?" Pop said with a laugh. "It was wartime, and they were anxious to ship us out. Maybe I should have taken an unauthorized practice jump like McClanahan. Anyway, I was floating backwards. The wind was blowing about thirty-five miles an hour, and when I hit the frozen ground backwards, that's when I injured my back and neck." He paused, stretching a little in his recliner.

"Then what?"

"Landed in a farmer's field. I couldn't release the parachute harness, so the wind dragged me on my back over the ground a hundred yards or so until the chute hit a fence and collapsed. I untangled myself from the chute and looked for a place to hide. Since I landed near the heavily fortified coast of France, German soldiers were coming in on all sides. There was no chance of escape. They forced me to pick up the chute and marched me into a small village nearby."

As a show of intimidation to the locals, the Germans routinely paraded their prisoners through town for all to see. My father's right hand had been injured by a shell fragment; blood dripped through his glove onto the ground. He described seeing French women with tears in their eyes and children lining both sides of the street, some of the children running alongside of him.

At the German Headquarters, my father was put under armed guard, and an Intelligence Officer was summoned to interrogate him.

"When he arrived, he asked me various questions, which I refused to answer, as we were trained to do," Pop told me. "The one question that disturbed me most was that he wanted to know how many men were aboard the plane, claiming that they found two bodies in the woods. He said that there may be more that were injured and in need of medical attention."

The officer claimed, "We have reports of several parachutes from your downed airplane, but you are the only one we have found. I need details on how many men bailed out of your airplane and who they are."

"Barney Wasowicz, Flight Officer, T120869," my father replied.

The officer went on, dramatically feigning concern for the men's well-being: "Your crew is still out there and no doubt badly wounded, and if we don't find them, and get them to a doctor, they will die."

"Barney Wasowicz, Flight Officer, T120869."

Pop told me, "I suspected that he was lying—especially since I myself had received no medical attention—but since I had no way of knowing if the three men in the rear of the plane got out, I was very worried. This was one of the tricks they used trying to find out if they had captured all of us."

"Sounds like you had a whole lot of practice saying your *name, rank, and serial number*," I commented.

"I was very grateful for our intelligence training," Pop nodded. "I kept second-guessing myself. What if the interrogator was telling the truth, and my crew members were not found? What if they were out there somewhere, injured and needing help?"

But Pop's rigorous conditioning prevailed. It was no use. The officer quickly perceived that this captive would never answer his questions, so he left him under guard.

"He left me alone after determining that I would be of no use to him," Pop said. "That ended the questions, and I waited, for what I later learned, was a truck to take us to another interrogation center in Frankfurt, Germany."

"That must have been a long wait," I said.

"It was," Pop agreed. "When the truck finally arrived, I can't tell you how relieved I was to see that, contrary to what the German officer had said, every man in my crew had been able to get out of the plane— McClanahan, Gemery, Carpenter, Fischer, and Higgins—they were all there in the back of the truck, badly injured but alive."

My father joined his crew, who were equally happy to see that Pop had made it out alive and relatively well. For 300 miles, they commiserated and tried to comfort each other, but they did not dare to discuss the details of the mission. They had been warned during training that many German soldiers understood English.

"I found out that Fischer, our engineer, and Carpenter, the radioman, had bailed out over the English Channel. A fifty-five-mile-per-hour wind carried them back over the enemy coast. Carpenter sprained an ankle in landing."

"What about Fischer?" I asked.

"He'd been wounded in both ankles by 20mm shrapnel," Pop recalled. "He told me that he could see German soldiers watching him come down. After hitting the beach, he tried to unlock his chute harness—it did not release when he turned the knob and struck it. Then he realized that he had jumped with the knob in the unlocked position! It was then that a German soldier walked up to him in a zigzag fashion. He spoke in clear English, 'Today is your second birthday. The entire beach is mined, we were waiting for you to blow up!'"

At the interrogation center in Frankfurt, the men were taken to a jailhouse with rows of mean little solitary cells. In the middle of winter, the prisoners, injured and traumatized, were each thrown into a five-by-eight-foot cell with a wood plank for a bed. No windows, no blankets. But this Hilton on the River Main did have room service: Their food ration, brought to them once a day, was a bowl of thin soup and some dark bread.

✈ ✈
✈ ✈
✈ ✈

The German Major's office was spacious, well-appointed, and very warm. It thawed my father's chilled bones and made him feel a little sleepy and weirdly happy. And the German Major was polite. Very polite. He offered my father a cigarette, which he gladly accepted, and invited him to sit in a comfortable chair. Evidently, my father had arrived at his *real* interrogation.

Like the first intelligence officer who had questioned my father, the Major asked him what type of plane he was flying, how many men were in his crew, bomb load, and other basic facts.

"Barney Wasowicz, Flight Officer, T120869," Pop replied.

A stern look. A long pause.

"I am sorry to hear that you will not help us." He tapped the bell on his desk. An armed guard entered the room and took my father away.

The temperature in my father's cell was *not* warm. Freezing, yes, roasting, yes. But never *warm*. On his first day in solitary, my father was slightly reassured to see an electric baseboard heater, only to realize that it was controlled from the hallway outside of the room.

"Every couple of hours, a guard would change the setting on the control back and forth between maximum and off," Pop told me. "This meant that it became so warm that I would have to strip all my clothes off, sweating, and a couple of hours later, so cold that I would have to put them back on again and shiver."

As the cruel little chambers alternated every few hours from meat locker to sauna, prisoners were unable to sleep or even relax. For seven days, my father and his crew were thus deprived of sleep, calories, and social interaction.

"This form of torture—if you can call it torture—is sleep deprivation and used to dull your thinking process and trick you into answering questions you normally wouldn't," Pop explained.

"I'm pretty sure that treatment can be called torture," I said, sickened at the thought of it.

The stultifying boredom was part of the torture. The prisoners were held under total solitary confinement, rarely getting even a glimpse of a guard.

My father found himself looking forward to his little chats with the Major, eagerly anticipating the respite, however brief, from the torment of his cell. Every day it was the same routine—big smile, comfortable chair, lighted cigarette, the polite inquiries about my father's plane, his crew, his bomb load, and so on—and the conditioned response:

"Barney Wasowicz, Flight Officer, T120869."

Pop recalled his addled state of mind: "After six days, I felt pretty proud of myself, enjoying the cigarette, thinking that this wasn't so bad!"

Then back to the lonely cell with its schizophrenic heater.

The time dragged by. He had a lot of time on his hands.

"What did you think about?" I asked.

"Well, the British Air Force bombed Frankfurt nightly, so I learned what it was like to be on the other end of the bombs I'd been dropping," Pop commented.

"What else?" I said. "Were you afraid that Babcia might not know that you were alive?"

"Of course, I was very concerned about that. A Red Cross Representative at the office told us that word of what had happened to us would be sent home, but I knew that could take a while. I pictured my mother's letters being returned to her, marked 'Missing.' This was her worst nightmare."

The task of sending official word of servicemen's status to their next of kin was the responsibility of the Adjutant General's office. On February 2, 1944, ten days after her only son's B-26 was shot down, Babcia received this telegram:

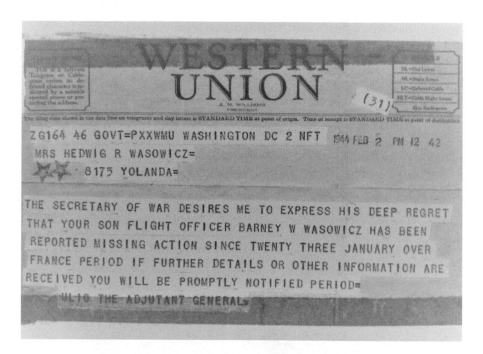

TELEGRAM FROM THE ADJUTANT GENERAL

"I was her only son," Pop said. "It seemed like a million years since I had last seen her—Babcia and I were taking the train together back to Detroit after the Pinning of the Wings Ceremony in Texas. That had been a proud moment for her even though she disapproved of my flying airplanes."

He paused and smiled ruefully. "In solitary, I thought of odd things. I thought about what I had decided was the most embarrassing moment of my military life."

"What happened?" I asked.

"During the war, travel by air was severely restricted, so the train was crowded with enlisted soldiers. I was looking for two seats so my mother and I could sit together. Here I was, a twenty-year-old, freshly minted officer, trying to cut a figure among all the seasoned veterans on the train. My brand-new officer's uniform was a little too big for me and still had the creases. While I was trying to look like a man and take charge, your grandmother

113

went to the rear of the car and shouted across the crowd of soldiers, 'Sonny, here's a seat!' You can just imagine how red my face must have been," he concluded, a little contritely.

Though I couldn't help laughing, I could see how painful it must have been for him, sitting in a prison cell halfway around the world, to think that his last memories of his mother were of disregarding her wishes, deceiving her, and then feeling embarrassed by her.

"Sorry, Pop," I said. "If it makes you feel any better, Mom embarrassed me lots of times. That's what moms do." He laughed a little at that and then closed his eyes. I thought he might be dozing off, so I sat quietly, reading my notes.

Graduation   Lubbock, Texas

POP AND BABCIA

"I turned the plane around," Pop said suddenly. "Should I have done that?"

I looked up.

"You're wondering how *I felt*," he continued sharply. "I *felt guilty*. I sat there in my cell all day and all night, feeling guilty, thinking about my crew. I had flown just over the English Channel when I turned the plane around and hit the bailout bell. The real torture of the solitary confinement was wondering if maybe I could've made it across and back to the base. At the time, I believed the plane was going to explode at some point, and I thought the crew would have a better chance at surviving this if I could get us closer to land. But that meant returning to enemy territory. I couldn't help wondering if I had made the right decision. Except for Gemery, all of us were badly wounded. And because of my decision, we were all prisoners of war."

He sat back and closed his eyes again.

"But you said yourself that the radio compartment was on fire, and the right side-engine was out, so—" He cut me off, smiling a little.

"I know, I know. Just listen."

I waited for him to continue.

"I carried that guilt with me for a long time," he went on after a moment. "Then, about thirty years after the war, I got a phone call, the sort of call that you wouldn't believe if it happened in a movie."

He paused.

"*I* couldn't believe it," Pop went on. "Out of the blue, the phone rings. 'Hello? Barney?' the caller says. 'For years I've been wanting to contact you and tell you one thing.'"

It was a member of the crew my father had valued so highly, one of the men who had bailed out of the rear of the airplane. He had tracked Pop down through Chester Klier, the Air Force Historian.

"Well, what did he say?" I asked impatiently.

"He told me that when he was parachuting down, before he landed, that he looked out into the sky and, in the distance, he saw our B-26 exploding in mid-air. It was shortly after he and the others got out. All these years, he'd been waiting to thank me. 'Thank you for saving my life,' he said."

Pop closed his eyes again, squeezing away the tears. I tried to speak but found I was unable to. It was the type of stuff you'd see in a movie and roll your eyes. But here we were. I could scarcely imagine how my father must have felt when he heard those reassuring words. It must have been a huge weight lifted off his tired, aching back.

After several minutes, Pop opened his eyes and said, "There was this other thing I thought about a lot—I couldn't stop picturing it in my mind. It was a memory from when I was just a little boy."

He had already told me about his childhood obsession, constantly drawing airplanes, playing pilot, and building models. But one day, he said, he took the game further.

"I don't know why I did it," he told me. "One day I built a real nice little airplane, took me all day, and I went up to the second story window to get the most altitude. Then I lit a match, touched it to the nose of the glider, and launched it. My most vivid memory of childhood is just standing and staring out the window as the flames engulfed the plane, and she took a nose-dive straight into the ground." He shook his head. "I thought about that a lot."

Pop looked suddenly shaken. "I still think about that."

Back at the interrogation center in Frankfurt, the German Major continued questioning the prisoners for six days. On the seventh day, once again relieved to be out of his cell for even a few minutes, my stressed-out father strutted into the Major's plush office and accepted his cigarette. Usual questions, usual answers.

"Barney Wasowicz, Flight Officer, T120869."

There was a long pause. My father took a deep drag on his cigarette.

"Then all heck broke loose!" Pop laughed.

The Major pounded on his desk and slapped the cigarette out of the prisoner's mouth. He was spitting mad. He threatened to hand him over to the Gestapo.

"The Gestapo knows how to get answers!" the Major shouted. He threw a chair across the room. "How dare you insult me like this?!" he screamed. My father could feel the heat of his breath just inches from his petrified face. "You are nothing! *Nothing!!!*" He went on for several minutes, in a furious rant, striding angrily across the large room only to return to yell in Pop's face again and again.

"Barney Wasowicz, Flight Officer, T120869," my father repeated mechanically.

Gradually the Major calmed down, his anger seemingly transformed into a kind of weary, disgusted resignation.

"It makes no difference what you say or do not say," he declared with a sneer. "We know more about you than you do." He sat down and tapped the bell to summon his secretary. She carried a big book into the room and placed it on the desk. It was labeled *386th Bomb Group*, like a photo album. The Major leaned forward and began to leaf through the pages in the book.

"Ah, here we are. Flight Officer Barney William Wasowicz, born in Detroit on 28 February 1922. Your father is dead. You have one sister, Wanda. You trained at Keesler Field at Biloxi, Mississippi."

The incomparable German spy system and their maniacal recordkeeping were on full display.

He went on for several minutes, listing the dates and locations of everything my father had done since he joined the Army: every school, every airbase, every commander, every crew member, every mission. Pop was stunned.

"They had my entire military history in it," he recalled, still amazed. "He even knew that my crew had replaced the one that was scheduled to fly the mission the day I was shot down. They knew more about me than my own mother!"

My father, flustered but determined, stared straight ahead, repeating, "Barney Wasowicz, Flight Officer, T120869."

The Major sighed, carefully closed the big book, and casually picked up the chair, returning it to its proper place.

"Guard!" he shouted. And with that, he dismissed my father from the room with a disdainful wave of his hand.

"Why would he ask you for information he already had and then throw it in your face?" I asked him.

"Theatrics," Pop explained. "The German spy system was the best in the world. In one of our briefings by British Intelligence, at our base in England, I had been warned to expect this sort of tactic. The whole purpose of this final act that he put on was to overwhelm me with how much he knew. This was supposed to lower my guard and possibly make me reveal something I thought of as unimportant during my interrogation. Any little bit of new information would add to the bigger picture."

Thus ended the bewildering and exhausting interrogation phase of the prisoners' captivity. But before they could leave Frankfurt, there was still more of the infamous German paperwork to be done. When the young German clerk at the desk noticed that my father was from Detroit, his face lit up.

"He had an American accent, so I asked him what he was doing in the German army," Pop recalled.

In fluent English, the young man informed Pop that he had been born in Germany but had grown up in the United States. Fatefully, he had been traveling to Germany with his parents just as war broke out. Because he was a German citizen by birth, he was drafted into the army. He and my father reminisced about the States for a bit, and then the clerk glanced around furtively and lowered his voice, saying, "I still know many people in New York. And I'm a little worried. How bad was it hit?"

Pop stared back, puzzled, for a moment. "How bad was *what* hit?"

"New York City, of course. The massive airstrike. I just read about it in the papers a few weeks ago. Most of the city must have been destroyed."

February 12, 1944,
8175 Yolanda Street,
Detroit, Michigan.

Dear Mrs. Wasowicz:-

Due to Army Regulations, it has been necessary for me to delay writing to you regarding your son who has been missing in action since 23 January 1944. In further review of Army policy, I must also convey that the information garnered in this letter is that of my own personal opinion and can in no way be considered as an official statement of the United States Army Air Forces.

On January 23ʳᵈ Flight Officer Wasowicz was flying on a mission against military installations in Northwest France. As our formation was leaving the enemy coast it was attacked by enemy fighters. The plane in which Flight Officer Wasowicz was flying was apparently severely damaged by cannon fire from the attacking fighters because it dropped out of formation and five parachutes were seen to open immediately. It is entirely possible that the remaining crew member escaped before the plane crashed as it entered the clouds long before it reached the ground and could no longer be seen by any of our personnel.

I have every reason to believe that Flight Officer Wasowicz escaped from the plane and that he is safe. He is either a prisoner of war or is making his way back to friendly territory at this time.

Flight Officer Wasowicz has always been held in the highest esteem by the officers and men of the Squadron and we join you in hoping for his safe and immediate return to our organization.

Charles V. Thornton
Major, Air Corps,
Commanding.

Major Thornton's letter provided cold comfort. For three weeks or more, my grandmother officially knew only that her son was "missing in action." But she was beginning to form an idea of what had happened. About a week after the letter from Major Thornton arrived, Babcia received this postcard:

We heard over short wave radio from Berlin this morning (Feb. 22nd) at 8:43 a.m. that Flying Officer Barney William Wasowicz is a prisoner of war of Germany.

We are organized to help you in any way we can. If you know the names of the other boys in your sons crew and would like to know if they have been heard or would like the parents addresses, we may have that information in our files. As you know this news comes from an enemy source but I have sent 900 cards and have not known of one to be false.

Mrs. Don Yant
Member of "Short Wave Amateur Monitors Club"
1175 Hazel Ave.
Lima, Ohio

This organization, I later learned, was no "amateur club." During the war, small groups of short-wave radio enthusiasts all over the world became a sounding board for any news they could pick up from the airwaves. At first, many of these listeners were random "lone wolf" hobbyists, but as the popularity of short-wave listening grew, underground organizations formed. One such organization was the Short-Wave Amateur Monitors Club—SWAM—a group of listeners organized by Mrs. Ruby Yant of Lima, Ohio. She must have been a remarkably dedicated woman. Each of her club's fifty members was assigned a specific night of the week to monitor the airwaves so that no intelligence would be missed. Records show that one member sent over 5,000 messages to families anxious for information about their missing loved ones.

While Babcia would have been extremely relieved to know that her son was alive, she must have been equally horrified to think of him languishing in a German POW camp. Sadly, I never thought to ask Babcia, who lived with my family when I was a boy, so I can only imagine the range of her emotions upon receiving this news from a kindhearted stranger in Ohio.

Evidently, the intelligence came from the Germans themselves, eager to "gloat over their conquests," as Pop told me. Not infrequently, short messages about prisoners of war were read by studio announcers at stations in Germany. In fact, the second telegram my grandmother received from the Adjutant General's office confirmed that this news came *"from an enemy source"*:

1944 FEB 22

THE NAME OF FLYING OFFICER BARNEY WILLIAM WASOWITZ HAS BEEN MENTIONED IN AN ENEMY BROADCAST AS A PRISONER IN GERMAN HANDS. THE PURPOSE OF SUCH BROADCASTS IS TO GAIN LISTENERS FOR THE ENEMY PROPAGANDA WHICH THEY CONTAIN: BUT THE ARMY IS CHECKING THE ACCURACY OF THIS INFORMA- TION AND WILL ADVISE YOU AS SOON AS POSSIBLE=

FOREIGN BROADCAST INTELLIGENCE SERVICE FEDERAL COMMUNICATIONS COMMISSION.

Interestingly, the masters of the most elite and cautious spy agency in the world thought nothing of announcing the names and addresses of the men they captured. Any shortwave radio listener could simply take down the information and then notify families by mail. My grandmother received at least seven such mailings from Pennsylvania, Virginia, New York, New Jersey, and of course the one from Mrs. Yant herself in Ohio. Some of these postcards added the poignant postscript, "Our son is also a POW." This practice became known as "Prisoner of War Relay."

It was puzzling to learn that these unsung heroes were the bane of the FBI. Because of a perceived threat to national security, it was illegal in both Germany and the United States for civilians to broadcast, via short wave radio, messages that could reach halfway around the world. Still, it was not a crime to *listen*, and as citizen activists like the members of SWAM secretly toiled underground to provide information to distraught families, the FBI was constantly trying to stop them, claiming that relaying the messages aided only the enemy. Nevertheless, even as the U.S. government attempted to provide the same type of service, the families usually heard from shortwave listeners first.

Meanwhile, the prisoners themselves were completely cut off from the kindness of strangers. They would have to wait many more weeks to have the solace of knowing that their loved ones had been notified of their whereabouts.

After one more night in the nerve-jangling little cell, my father was put into a railroad boxcar, bound for Barth, Germany, on the coast of the Baltic Sea. He and his Co-pilot Harold McClanahan and the Bombardier-Navigator Matt Gemery were sent to *Stalag Luft I*, over 300 miles to the north. The rest of the crew—Bob Carpenter, Engineer; Bud Fischer, Radio Operator; and Lester Higgins, Tail-gunner—were sent to different prison camps across Germany.

Pop never saw them again.

386TH BOMB GROUP, COLCHESTER, ENGLAND, 1943
F/O BARNEY WASOWICZ, PILOT; F/O HAROLD MCCLANAHAN, CO-
PILOT; LT. MATT GEMERY, BOMBARDIER; S/SGT. BOB CARPENTER,
RADIOMAN; S/SGT. LOUIS FISCHER, ENGINEER; S/SGT. LESTER
HIGGINS, TAIL GUNNER.

CHAPTER 10

Stalag Luft I

I was taken to a Dutch hospital, and after a time I was transferred to Dulag for interrogation, eighteen days of solitary, and a lot of name, rank, and serial number. They showed me their intelligence book on the 386th Bomb Group. Everything was there except where we were stationed, which I never told them. All they wanted to do they said, was show me that I wasn't so smart because they had all that information anyway! They needed my cell, so I was shipped off to Barth, Germany, via the Berlin marshalling yards—during an air raid!

—Captain R.P. Sanford

Situated on the northern outskirts of Barth, a small village on the Baltic Sea, *Stalag Luft I* was a German prisoner-of-war camp for captured Allied airmen. The camp was originally built to house around 500 men, but its numbers grew rapidly, unimaginably, beyond capacity. When Russian troops liberated the camp in April 1945, nearly 9,000 airmen—7,588 American and 1,351 British and Canadian—were being held at the camp.

Three long, cold days after departing the interrogation center in Frankfurt, the prisoner transport truck pulled up to *Stalag Luft I*, and the prisoners were marched through the prison camp gates.

"When I entered the camp, the first person I saw was Captain Ray Sanford," my father began.

"Wait," I said. "You mean the Captain Sanford whose plane was blown to pieces during the Schiphol mission?"

"That's right," Pop said. "It was like seeing a ghost. I was stunned, couldn't say a word. Everyone assumed that no one survived the explosion since no parachutes were spotted. Sanford said that the only thing he remembered was, one minute he was flying over the target, and the next minute he was falling through the air, still strapped in his seat."

Many crews from that mission reported seeing the flaming wreckage of HELL'S FURY go down. Every man in the bomber group had witnessed the horrific explosion; later, the photograph verified it—clearly, no one could have survived that direct hit.

Pop showed me a copy of the de-briefing notes that Sanford made following his liberation. Sanford's recollection of the event was jaw-dropping:

The ground gunners all concentrated on our box. They already had altitude and speed from the first boxes. The flak was so thick you could have walked on it! All I really remember was the hit and immediate loss of control. I think I radioed, "We're going down," but I'm not sure, it all happened so fast.

I was knocked out apparently, so I don't know if Jackson had time to hit the salvo button. We were so close to bomb release point, everyone was eager to get the hell out of there! I revived in mid-air still strapped in my seat, with my right arm just floating free; I had no use of it. I didn't know then, but my right shoulder must have struck the airplane structure that separates the pilot and co-pilot hatches—my collarbone was broken.

Discipline is a strange thing, I wasn't scared. The first thing I thought of was some jump instructor telling the class, if you turn your head you roll—put out your legs for control, etc. I was going to try it out until I could see the ground closing in. I tried to drop the seat left-handed, but my jacket was over the belt, so I had to pull the rip cord left-handed, some trick! I leaned forward in the seat so the backpack would open, it did, and the seat really put a jerk on my legs. While dropping I released the seat and I just seemed to hang there after the sudden loss of the extra 300 plus pounds of pilot seat and armor plate.

Some Dutch were outside the fence with a car, but I couldn't control the chute with only the use of one hand. I landed on the target airdrome about 200 feet from the fence and about 150 feet in front of a German barracks, then the occupants in the Dutch car sped off! I became an instant POW. I wasn't hit by flak, but co-pilot Roberts must have been, my whole right side was flecked with white. I think we must have had two simultaneous flak hits—the left wing and also the fuselage under the waist or turret, but I am not sure. During the explosion the aircraft broke up into several large pieces.

"Captain Sanford's dramatic experience was just one of many I heard during my imprisonment," Pop told me. "It seemed that 9,000 men each had their own story to tell. Their stories usually began, 'There I was, upside down, at twenty-thousand feet....'"

More remarkable still, the only reason Captain Sanford survived was that he was wearing an illegal parachute. At the airfield before his fateful mission, Captain Sanford was in the process of starting his engines when an officer ran up, waving a handful of papers. The pilot pulled his throttles back and slid open the side cockpit window to find out what it was all about. The man shouted, "These are your court-martial papers!" Sanford ignored the officer as he released his brakes—it was time to taxi out. The man yelled after him, "Just wait until you get back!" This threat of a court-martial resulted from a new regulation that strictly forbade the use of their usual American parachutes in favor of the newer British chutes. Captain Sanford preferred the American version because it was thin enough to wear in-flight. The British version was bulky, and in the case of the pilot, was stored behind his seat in the tiny navigation compartment. Somehow the Commanders had caught wind of his transgression and were not sympathetic. Rules are rules, after all, especially in wartime. Undeterred and going against direct orders, Captain Sanford was the only man to leave the base that day with an illegal parachute. It saved his life. His only significant injury was a broken collarbone.

"The seatbelt straps caused the injury because he didn't release the seat before pulling the ripcord to open the chute," Pop explained.

The rest of Sanford's HELL'S FURY crew weren't so lucky. Only two men survived, albeit briefly. Lieutenant Charles Jackson had come down in the wreckage of the nose section; he lived until December 23, 1943. Staff Sergeant Herbert King also lost his chute pack during the breakup of the aircraft and went down in the tail cone section. The Sergeant died of his injuries on Christmas Day 1943.

Pop paused, still grieving the loss of those men. I tried to comprehend how anyone could survive, even briefly, such a free fall in burning wreckage.

"What about medical care?" I said. "Was there any help for all of those injured men?"

"No," he said, shaking his head. "The promised medical attention was a lie. Not one of my crew had seen a doctor before we got into the camp, even though some were badly wounded. There were prisoners with medical experience, of course, and they tried to help as much as they could, but there were virtually no supplies, and conditions were very unsanitary."

He gave me the rundown on the condition of his crew: "As I told you, Bob Carpenter sprained his ankle and had several shell fragments, nothing serious. Bud Fischer had a 20mm armor piercing shell go through both ankles, luckily missing the tendons. Les Higgins had both arms badly damaged by a shell which exploded between his twin .50 caliber guns. Les never did regain full use of his arms. Matt Gemery survived uninjured except for a little singeing of his mustache."

"Amazing," I said. "Wasn't he the one in the nosecone?"

"That's right. It *was* amazing that Gemery wasn't hurt, especially considering that the fire had burned the bungee cords off of his chute pack, which had been stowed in the radio compartment. Remember I told you? Harold McClanahan's neck and ears were badly burned while he was retrieving Gemery's parachute, plus he was hit with shell fragments in his back. Gemery actually jumped with his unattached chute pack clutched in his arms!"

I just shook my head. After a moment, I asked him about his own injuries.

"I had shell fragments in my hand and shoulder," he began. "My right hand was infected and had blown up like a balloon. Fortunately, there were three British doctors, captured in South Africa. Once I got into camp, they removed the flak and a piece of the glove that I wore at the time, but they had only very primitive equipment. And no medicines. They did the best they could, under the circumstances."

Now he stretched his right hand and made a gnarled fist. He had suffered arthritis for as long as I could remember.

"It could have been worse," he said.

+ +
+ +
+ +

It was difficult for me to fathom the scale of the place. *Nine thousand men?*

"But where did all those men live and sleep? And eat and bathe? What did the camp look like? How was it all organized?" I asked, wide-eyed.

Pop smiled at my astonishment. "It was a typical prison camp, kind of like the ones you see in the movies: wooden barracks enclosed by barbed wire, patrolled inside and out by guards with dogs. For us, the camp operated like any other military base—the highest-ranking officer among us was in charge of the camp, in this case a colonel, and so on down the line of command."

Surrounded by miles of barbed wire attached to tall posts, *Stalag Luft I* was divided into five separate compounds, four for prisoners, and one for their German captors. Of course, the German buildings and quarters were well constructed and attractively landscaped. In stark contrast, the prisoners lived in crowded ramshackle barracks that were inadequate in every way. My father's barrack consisted of eight rooms—nineteen men to a room. The triple bunkbeds had no springs, just wires stretched on a metal frame. The "mattress" was a scratchy burlap bag filled with straw.

"After a couple of nights, you could feel each of the wires strung under the straw, so it had to be fluffed out again," Pop recalled.

The only space that a man could call his own was his bunk. He had no locker, not so much as a box. At interrogation, the Swedish Red Cross provided each man one blanket, one pair of pants, one shirt, and one pair of shoes. And a safety razor with one blade. Other than that, each man had only the clothes he was wearing when he walked through the gate.

"One razor?" I said, recalling war movies I'd seen in which the POWs were usually clean shaven.

"Naturally, I didn't shave very often!" Pop said with a laugh. "After shaving a couple of times, I would hone the razor blade on a glass window, but it was still pretty dull."

The barracks themselves were mere shacks and simply not fit for human habitation. Many of the buildings were not even weather proofed; during the extremely cold winter of northern Germany, living conditions were practically unbearable. Both the number of stoves and the amount of fuel issued were totally insufficient to maintain even minimal health. In the crowded conditions, upper respiratory diseases were rampant, becoming even worse when the Germans commanded the men to keep the shutters closed during the night, preventing fresh air from circulating.

The most serious detriment to the health of the men at *Stalag Luft I* was the appalling lack of sanitation. Detailed accounts of the conditions vary, but no one disputes that the compounds were deplorably deficient. No real facilities existed for the disposal of garbage, which was strewn about, attracting all manner of vermin. Each building had only one toilet and one wash basin, and the plumbing of the latrine and wash basin drains was so shoddy that the areas around the barracks were frequently flooded with wastewater.

Amid the filthy surroundings, it was impossible for the men to keep themselves clean. Over 4,000 officers were assigned to one bathing facility, a single bathhouse containing just ten showerheads. Worse, the bathhouse was also used as a delousing plant for new arrivals or for any outbreaks of body-crawling insects. Once a week, one group at a time would be marched outside the compound to the shower building, a large open room with shower heads spaced about six feet apart. The men were ordered to strip and stand under a shower head for a cold three-minute shower.

I winced as Pop recited the process: "Four men per shower head. The water would be turned on for one minute, allowing us to get wet, and then shut off. We had one minute to soap up, if we had any, and then the water would be turned on again for another minute to rinse the soap off. I don't think we ended up much cleaner than when we started, but at least it was something."

"What about laundry?" I asked.

"No laundry system at all. I would rinse my shirt periodically, and when that was dry, I would rinse my pants."

So, these unwashed men wore unwashed clothes because of the shortage of wash basins and soap. I shook my head as I imagined all these grimy men walking around prison camp in just their shirt or pants.

"The only good thing about the prison camp was that the interrogation phase was over," Pop told me. "Once you were in the camp, you were no longer of any use to them."

For the most part, these tough young soldiers bore their hardships patiently. It seems their biggest challenge was the excruciating boredom. My father recalled the scene on the day he arrived at *Luft I*:

"I was a little worried as I approached the gate and could see the condition of the prisoners inside. It was shocking. Some were crawling on the ground, others holding on to the barbed wire fence for support and crying out in pain."

"Really?" I said, appalled.

"I later learned that they were just joking around," Pop laughed.

No matter how bad things get, Americans never seem to lose their sense of humor. Even morbid humor.

At *Stalag Luft I*, the tedium was intensified by the fact that the camp was built to house only captured *officers*, not enlisted men. Per the Geneva Conventions, commissioned officers could not be forced to work at non-war-related jobs while imprisoned.

"Germany abided by some of the rules, and this was one of them," Pop explained. "This turned out to be a mixed blessing for officers. Since the enlisted men could work, the Germans fed them a halfway decent diet in order to keep them productive. On the other hand, we officers were of no use to the Germans, so they did no more than they had to for us."

Perhaps even worse, officers were also deprived of any relief from the monotony of prison life.

"What did you do all day?" I asked.

"The daily routine was always the same," Pop said. "Fall out for roll call every morning, back in the barracks at dark. During the day, we were on our own, free to wander around the compound. Mostly we talked about food."

Talking about food was not the whole story of course.

A large pine forest bordered the west side of the camp and, to the east and north, the waters of Barth Harbor lapped against the shore less than a mile from the barbed wire fence. Within the barbed wire enclosure, guard towers, placed every hundred yards, loomed over the camp with machine guns and spotlights ensuring unobstructed views of all activity within the confines of the enclosure. Guards with dogs constantly patrolled the perimeter, inside and out.

Barbed wire, constant surveillance, guards with dogs and machine guns. I imagined the prisoners must have been in a constant state of terror. But according to my father—in the beginning at least—the worst parts were just the monotony and hunger. Since the POWs had nothing to do all day except dream about food, they had plenty of time for their favorite diversion—trying to get out.

"We were always trying to figure a way out, and our best chance would be by digging a tunnel," Pop explained. "The way to accomplish this was to raise a couple of floorboards in our room, drop into the crawl space beneath, and start digging toward the fence."

"It sounds a lot like *Hogan's Heros* on T.V.," I joked.

"Actually, the show wasn't very far off. It just wasn't as funny in real life," he clarified. "We had all become quite adept at constructing the tools we needed from KLIM cans."

"Wait," I said, interrupting the story. "What the heck is a *KLIM can?*"

"Spell it backwards!" Pop said, laughing.

KLIM, I learned, is a brand of powdered milk still sold worldwide today. Developed in 1920, it is a dehydrated whole-milk powder for use in the tropics, where fresh milk tends to spoil quickly. During World War II, the Red Cross issued KLIM to German POW camps to give prisoners desperately needed calories. But the containers were as valuable as the contents. The empty cans could be fashioned into a variety of different tools and other useful items such as pots, scoops, candle holders—and shovels. They were also fitted together to construct airtight pipes to provide air while digging escape tunnels.

"We also used the cans for the dirt brigade," he said. "That was the hardest part, figuring out what to do with all the dirt we dug up."

To the prisoners, tunnel-digging was an art form, and everybody pitched in. To create any chance of escape, digging a tunnel had to be a tightly coordinated effort. Just like in the movies, a carefully orchestrated set of men would methodically dispose of the soil from the digging.

Pop described the process: "As the man digging at the head of the tunnel filled a can with dirt, it would be passed back, man to man, and then scattered over the crawl space."

Other times, over and over, slowly but steadily, the men would fill a pants pocket or two with the excavated dirt, casually stroll the yard for a bit, lean up against a building or fencepost and light a cigarette, and slowly let it drain through a tiny hole in the pocket. This was not a fast process. Nor a successful one.

"The major problem we encountered was that the guards had seismographs planted around the perimeter of the camp," Pop continued. "When a tunnel reached the fence, the guards were able to locate the source and stage a raid."

In addition to the seismographs around the perimeter of the camp, the barracks themselves were raised on posts, so it was easy to send guard dogs underneath the floorboards and detect signs of tunneling. Diabolically, the guards would often discover a tunnel but let the digging continue for a week or so before destroying it. A typical game of cat and mouse. Perhaps they figured they might as well keep the prisoners busy with a known tunnel, as long as they didn't make it past the fence. Each thwarted attempt was a blow to the POWs' morale—it always seemed they had come so close.

"By the time we were liberated by the Russian Army, a total of 140 tunnels had been dug, none successful. No one got out," Pop recalled.

I was surprised by both the large number and his precise memory.

My father recounted the one time they almost made it.

"One of our group came up with a new approach. Why not build *two* tunnels at the same time, near each other, and camouflage only one?" Pop laughed. "This way, when the Germans discovered and collapsed the one tunnel, they wouldn't think to look any further."

"Good thinking!" I said.

"Yes, it was! And it worked just as planned. The guards found the tunnel, collapsed it, and left. The next night, we finished the second tunnel and made our preparations to escape."

Ultimately, *The Great Escape* this was not. As fate would have it, when the first man popped his head out of the ground outside the fence, he found himself directly between a patrolling guard taking a smoke break and the machine gunner in the guard tower. My father was one of several men inside the tunnel, lying on his belly in the dark, waiting for his turn to get out.

"The guard walking outside the fence had stopped to talk to the guard in the tower," Pop recalled. "The tower guard's line of sight was directly toward the exit of the tunnel. He immediately sounded the alarm and several of us were caught in the tunnel before we could get out."

"What if you had managed to escape?" I asked. "Then what? Where would you have gone?"

Pop laughed ruefully. "Well," he said, "the main thing was to get out. But that was only half the battle. It would have been extremely difficult to reach Allied lines because the camp was so deep in Germany. My plan was to head in the other direction toward Poland. I could speak Polish, so I thought I might be able to connect with the Polish underground. But of course, I never got the chance. All I got from that attempt was another seven days in solitary confinement."

"It was a great day when I got back to my room in the barrack after seven days in solitary," Pop recalled with pleasure. "My share of the food had been saved for me."

"Your roommates must have been pretty tempted to dip into your rations," I commented.

"Maybe," he said doubtfully. "But I think our loyalty to one another was stronger. Anyway, when I got back, I also learned that the long-awaited invasion of France by our troops had taken place."

Recalling the young clerk in Frankfurt who had believed Nazi propaganda saying that the Germans had destroyed New York City, I asked my father how the POWs had gotten reliable news of the war.

"Well, we learned a lot from the new arrivals at camp, of course. But we learned even more from the BBC!" he grinned.

Boredom breeds ingenuity. Sealed off from the world, the POWs yearned for news from home and factual updates on the Allied war effort. Many of the officers were college educated, trained engineers who had nothing to do all day.

So, they decided to build a radio.

Not to be confused with the terrifying *SS* or murderous *Gestapo*, the *Stalag* guards responsible for the airmen were mainly retired *Luftwaffe*, the aerial warfare branch of the German armed forces, so they were courteous to the officers, if not collegial. They adhered to the Geneva Conventions, treating their prisoners accordingly. As the war went on, most of the guards were gradually replaced with the "Home Guard," older men who would have preferred to stay home. These conscripted men were just happy not to be on the frontlines. Like their prisoners, they were also battling the interminable tedium of the camp. They spoke some English, and they would converse with the prisoners to pass the time. But friendly conversation was as far as it went. It was death by firing squad for guards caught trading goods with prisoners—no exceptions. Along with the powerful currency of American cigarettes, the POWs used this brutal directive to procure parts for a radio.

"A few of our men who could speak fluent German were selected to be the official traders," Pop recalled. "These guys had a certain knack. And nobody else was allowed to trade. We didn't want anyone to screw it up."

Traders were experts at befriending hand-picked guards and slowly gaining their trust. After weeks or months of grooming, when the time was right, the trader would offer to swap the guards some good American cigarettes for something very small and innocuous. With persistence and some luck, he might get it.

"The articles they traded for, at first, were trivial," Pop continued. "An onion today, an egg next week, and so on. After a while, copper wire was added to the requests, and a little at a time, other small items that were needed to assemble a radio."

The trader would say that the item was needed to repair something like a wood stove or shoe. Each time, the trade would be for something more substantial.

"When it came to the stage where the radio tubes or other vital parts were needed, the guard would realize the trader was trying to build a radio, and say '*Nein!* You are building a radio!'" Pop told me. "The trader would then lower the boom and threaten to take the half-built radio to the camp *Kommandant* and report the guard if he did not comply. Like I said, punishment for guards trading with prisoners was death by firing squad. Needless to say, the parts were soon delivered."

So eventually, they had a working radio. And the Germans knew it. But although they foiled every escape attempt, their captors never did find the radio.

"Only four or five men knew the location of the radio," Pop explained. "As with the tunnel-digging, they had spies on guard at all times who would warn them when the Germans were staging one of their 'surprise raids.' Meanwhile, the Germans continued giving us reports as to how the war was progressing, and naturally they claimed that Germany was advancing on all fronts, and they were winning the war."

After hearing the entertaining tall tales of German domination, the few men who were party to the radio would sit up late listening to the BBC and learning the facts, the most pertinent of which were first hand-written, then typed on small sheets of paper.

"Several copies were then printed on the home-made press and then passed from hand-to-hand throughout the camp. Then of course they had to be burned," Pop explained.

"You had a *printing press*?" I asked in disbelief. "How on earth did you manage that?"

"To be honest, I don't have any idea how the printing press was constructed," he admitted, laughing. "But each barrack got a carbon copy of the BBC news, delivered in the false bottom of a KLIM can. It was a great morale booster when we got to read the real news."

I later learned that this little operation was in fact Germany's largest underground newspaper. It was called the *POW WOW—Prisoners of War Waiting on Winning*—and it was printed from May 1944 to May 1945. Reliably transcribing the news from the BBC, this paper became a "two-sheeter." It even had an eight-page Sunday supplement.

POW WOW

THE ONLY TRUTHFUL NEWSPAPER IN GERMANY

TO BE READ SILENTLY, QUICKLY AND IN GROUPS OF THREE

Amazingly, in its frequent portrayals of POW camps, Hollywood had gotten many of the details right: the barbed wire, the gullible guards, the ingenious inventions, the gallows humor, the deep loyalty, the indomitable spirit. Still, I knew in my bones that these men had been hungry and cold, lonely and frightened. They had reason to despair. And it haunted me.

CHAPTER 11

Ersatzbrot

The belly is an ungrateful wretch, it never remembers past favors, it always wants more tomorrow.

—Aleksandr Solzhenitsyn
One Day in the Life of Ivan Denisovich

Just before going to Europe, I went to see my father again. He had lost weight and some of his vitality since I last saw him, and he said he didn't want to go to the dining room; he was now taking his meals in his apartment at Silver Springs. After we finished supper, I made some green tea, and we settled down in his small sitting room.

"Do you want some of this pie they brought us?" I asked him. "I'm sure it's not as good as your famous Dutch apple pie, but it looks decent. I'll heat it up for you."

"No, thank you," he said. "Maybe later."

It seemed like a good time to ask him about the food at *Stalag Luft I*.

The scarcity of food that the men had endured at the Base Camp in England was nothing compared to the starvation diet they subsisted on in prison camp. The routine, at first, was always the same. Every other week, the Germans would deliver the meager food and fuel rations to the center of the compound, leaving distribution of the supplies to the men. The men would divide it equally among the barracks; each barrack would divide it among the rooms; and the men in each room would then decide how they wanted to apportion their share.

"In our room," Pop explained, "we decided to pool everything, rationing out so much each day, hoping it would last until the next batch came in. But in some cases, the men tried to take care of their own share."

"Why didn't you do that?" I asked, not seeing his point.

"Well, if you had your own food, it was too tempting to cheat. The men with little willpower would end up with nothing to eat for a couple of days."

"Gotcha," I agreed, remembering many a long backpacking trip that had ended that way.

"Everybody talked about food, all the time," he went on. "Nobody talked about family or the girl back home. We talked about food, our favorite dishes we had back home."

I nodded, again recalling the last day of a typical backpacking trip, fantasizing about food all the way back to the parking lot.

"The first couple months of the sixteen months I was imprisoned weren't quite so bad—not like how it got in the end," Pop continued. "It was the parcels that made all the difference."

"Parcels?"

"The food that kept us alive came from the Red Cross. They furnished what were called 'Red Cross Parcels.' These parcels were designed to provide enough nutrition to keep one man alive for a week."

Somehow, although food was scarce everywhere during the war, the Red Cross managed to deliver enough provisions to keep the far-flung POWs alive. At the beginning of my father's internment, the Red Cross boxes were issued at the rate of one per person per week. This food was distributed by the barracks blocks, each barrack receiving one-third of its total weekly parcels three days a week. The exact contents of the boxes, I learned, varied, but always included cans of meats and fish and vegetables, as well as bread, coffee, sugar, soap, Vitamin C tablets, toothpaste, undershirts, and more.

When I read Pop the list on the website of the "official" contents of those Red Cross parcels, he chuckled.

"That might have been what *was* in the box. That's not what we got." He closed his eyes and thought about it for a moment, as if visualizing opening one of those precious parcels years ago.

"One can KLIM,

"One can of meat—corned beef or Spam,

"One package of crackers,

"One piece of strong cheese,

"One bar of dark baking chocolate."

I waited for more. There was a long pause and then he opened his eyes.

"That's it?!" I cried.

"Oh, that's right," he said. "A pack of cigarettes. We also got a pack of cigarettes."

"Very nutritional," I said, nodding. "What happened to the rest of the stuff?"

Pop just laughed. "The Germans pilfered them, of course, especially toward the end of the war. They censored our letters, and they stole our food."

In the end, nearly 1.4 million American and Allied Prisoners of War in Germany and elsewhere were grateful beneficiaries of Red Cross services during World War II. Some 13,500 volunteers assembled the packages at chapters in the U.S. for shipment to Geneva, Switzerland, for distribution in the POW camps. Over 27,000,000 parcels were distributed to American, British, Belgian, French, Polish, Yugoslav, Netherlands, Greek, Norwegian, and Russian prisoners of war.

"I just sent them another check," Pop told me. "They saved my life. Every time I received Red Cross provisions in prison camp, I vowed that someday I would pay them back."

Aside from the Red Cross parcels, the men had to rely on whatever their captors could scrounge up to keep them alive. Pop reminded me that he was in an Officers Camp, and unlike enlisted men, they were not allowed to work. Not only did this "privilege" make camp life tedious, but it also gave the

Nazis an excuse to feed the men only a subsistence diet. As was the case for most of the rest of Europe during the war, there just wasn't much food available in Germany.

Except for rutabagas.

"The only food the Germans provided was barley, a little dark bread, occasionally some horse meat, and rutabagas," according to Pop.

Before my conversations with my father, I had no idea that this humble vegetable, a cross between the cabbage and the turnip, was the staple of the POW diet. When I was growing up, my mom never, *ever* cooked rutabagas. Now I knew why. As an adult, I had become an avid gardener and foodie, so I was curious about this large, purple and yellow root I had seen occasionally at supermarkets but had never tasted. A bit of research revealed that the lowly rutabaga had a long connection with war. The third winter of WWI, between 1916-17, is referred to in German as *Steckrübenwinter*—Rutabaga winter. At this time, the Allied blockade of Germany through the North Sea cut the country off from overseas trade and supplies. And worse, the potato crop had failed, leaving nothing much to eat other than rutabagas, which were grown mainly to feed cattle. Growing rutabagas was cheap and easy. During the fall, livestock would graze on the rutabaga tops; in winter, the animals would feed on the oversized roots. To be clear, the type, quality, and age of rutabagas in those times were not at all the same as the often-times delicious and nutritious root vegetable you may find at your local farmers' market today. These roots were animal fodder, a food of last resort for famished people. But these were desperate times. The great German singer and actress Marlene Dietrich, who was then a teenager in Berlin, would recall with a shudder how her family ate rutabagas, in every possible form, for breakfast, lunch, and dinner, to the extent that people's faces turned yellow from the pigment in the root. The dire situation was much the same years later during the second World War.

"Truckloads of them," Pop recalled with a grimace.

About once a week, the gates of *Stalag Luft I* would creak open, and an old supply truck, loaded with football-sized rutabagas, would drive into camp, dump the load in the center, and drive off. The hungry men gathered them off the ground, divided them up, and carried them to the barracks. Food was prepared by the men in their own barrack.

"How did you cook them?" I asked.

"Well, we had to boil them a long time, of course, just to make them edible and make the broth. The Germans gave us a weekly ration of charcoal, which we saved for cooking because there was not enough to use for heating the room. Remember what I told you about how important the KLIM cans were? One of the men came up with the idea of making a blower to conserve our supply of charcoal. He constructed a fan out of one of the cans, a set of pulleys out of others, and shoelaces for pulley belts. We dug up some clay for the pot to hold the charcoal. This system worked so well that we could bring a gallon of water to the boiling point, using just one coal!"

"Impressive!" I said, truly impressed. "What did you use for pots and pans?"

"As a matter of fact, I was named the official pot maker for our room," Pop declared proudly. "I became quite adept at constructing pots and pans by joining the empty, quart-sized KLIM cans together."

"No kidding! How did you do it?"

"Well, I didn't have any tools, of course, but the Germans issued each of us one set of eating utensils and a plate. So I used a table knife and a rock to form watertight joints. You'd be surprised at what you can accomplish with what you have on hand! We used these pots to cook the rutabagas and barley and what other little food we had."

"Incredible," I said, wondering what the Germans thought of these ingenious, resourceful men they were holding in conditions not fit for livestock.

As in the *Steckrübenwinter*, rutabagas again became a survival food. The situation was even worse for POWs since their rations were cut monthly, and their Red Cross parcels were routinely looted.

At least rutabagas were technically a *food*.

"Along with the rutabagas, we were sometimes given a ration of *ersatz*," Pop added.

This was another "food" I'd never heard of that turned out to be even more unappetizing.

He laughed and answered my puzzled expression. "Ersatz looked a lot like a dark brown loaf of bread, but it was really mostly sawdust."

Like rutabagas, ersatz had come into infamy during WWI. Its exotic name is borrowed from the German word for *substitute* or *replacement*. Generally, *ersatz* refers to a host of things that the Germans had to develop a substitute for, including synthetic rubber. "Tea" was composed of ground raspberry or catnip leaves, and it was ground roasted acorns or beans that were in that hot cup of Joe. What my father and his fellow prisoners were eating was *Ersatzbrot*, made of potato starch and sawdust, the same counterfeit food rationed to prisoners in Nazi labor and death camps.

When I asked Pop if he ever got any fresh meat, he shook his head. "During my first few months in the camp, a couple of cats were seen wandering around. Boy, did they pick the wrong place at the wrong time!"

I stared at him.

"Oh, don't look at me like that," he said. "I personally did not eat any cats. But I talked to others who did, and they said it tasted like rabbit."

Pop never did acquire a taste for rabbit.

"Once in a while, we did have horsemeat," he continued. "About once a month, the guards would drag the carcass of a horse into camp for us to distribute. As you can imagine, we were all very excited. The men with butcher experience carved it up and we all got a tiny taste, about a two-inch cube, maybe. But what I really remember, what I can never forget, is what happened later on one day. I walked around the corner of a barrack and surprised a POW standing there in the shadows. He was gnawing on a tiny piece of horse bone. He saw me and gave me a look like a starving stray dog, a look that said, 'Don't come near me and don't even think about taking my bone.' He would have growled if he could. I'll never forget that look."

Another story was a bit more humorous, if no less appalling. During his entire imprisonment my father had never once received a package from home. Nor did anyone else. Packages were no doubt sent but could never make it past the hungry German guards. Except once. One day, somehow, a package from home made it through to a man in Pop's room. And to everyone's astonishment and glee, it was a box of the man's favorite candy bar—the Baby Ruth. The generous soldier divvied up the contents, giving each man in the room his own bar. But elation quickly turned to revulsion as the men discovered why, this time, the Germans had delivered this box to its rightful owner. The candy bars were completely covered in tiny, wriggling worms.

"We were devastated," Pop recalled.

But shortly after light's out, in the total darkness, there could be heard the crinkling sound of a candy wrapper being opened. And then the sound of somebody chewing. Then, one by one, each man followed suit, contentedly munching his share, the worms out of sight and out of mind.

"Not being able to see what we eating, to us they were just Babe Ruth bars. Delicious," Pop said without a hint of irony.

After D-Day, the food shortage went from dire to desperate. In the beginning, the standard ration of food in *Stalag Luft I* provided 1200 to 1800 calories per man. But starting in October of 1944, little by little, the ration dwindled to around 800 calories. This coincided with a drastic drop in the delivery of Red Cross parcels.

"By the time we were liberated by the Russian Army, we were receiving only one parcel a month instead of one a week," Pop told me. "We could hardly blame the Germans—after all, our Air Force destroyed most of their railroads and other means of transportation."

Supplies were low everywhere; shipping lanes were in chaos, and even if a box got in, there were plenty of very hungry German hands it would have to pass through. During the entire month of March 1945, no parcels at all were distributed, and German rations were shrinking alarmingly. Toward the end of the month, some of the men became so weak that they would fall on the floor while attempting to get out of their beds. The strongest prisoners stood guard around garbage cans to prevent the worse off from eating the rubbish and becoming sick.

In early April, just weeks before the camp was liberated, a shipment finally came through to save the day, another example of the tireless efforts of the International Red Cross.

To generate heat and maintain a healthy, comfortable core temperature, the human body has to burn a certain number of calories. Throughout my father's imprisonment, he was in a constant state of hunger and cold. Even after being liberated from prison camp and returning home, he suffered the side effects of malnutrition he endured while imprisoned in Germany: low body temperature, headaches, dysentery, gum disease, constant fatigue. He dealt with these troubles for the rest of his life.

"After the war," Pop declared to me, "I promised myself that I would never again eat bad food. That I would pay more attention to food. That I would appreciate it and eat only the best food. And no fast food." ·

And, scarred from harsh winters in prison camp on a starvation diet of cold rations, Pop always insisted his food be served piping hot. He would even warm up dinner plates and soup bowls in the oven before putting steaming hot food into them. Still, I don't think he ever had a bowl of soup or a cup of coffee that was hot enough.

My father truly loved and appreciated food. Maybe more than anyone I've ever known. He taught me that food is life.

It was in the final weeks of his life that he told me, seemingly out of the blue, "I always thought that someday, if I ever I lost my love of good food, it would be my time to go." He paused. "Nothing tastes or sounds good anymore."

CHAPTER 12

A Few Postcards

My Uncle Bob was a first pilot. He told me he had two close calls, but I never pressed him, he never talked about it. He passed away never telling what happened on those two missions. So many questions not asked and answered but that's normal. I've had close relationships with a few Marauder Men, and they answered every question I asked, but then they pass away, and every single time I tell myself, "Damn, I should have asked him." It must be normal because as I lost my friends, I seemed to always have unanswered questions.

—Mike Smith, Founder, Martin B-26 Marauder Website

"The happiest times of my life were the years building the place in Rosita," Pop announced, just when I thought he'd drifted off to sleep. Daylight was fading, and he seemed to be tired of talking about war. I put down my pen.

"Building that cabin was the craziest and greatest thing you ever did, Pop," I said, and we sank into reverie.

The town of Rosita—little rose—was the idyllic setting of my father's dream house. He built it himself after he moved the family from the crowded concrete city of Detroit to the juniper dotted prairie outside of Pueblo, Colorado. Rosita was a silver town and, starting in 1872, briefly attracted a surge of prospectors. At its peak, the rush drew in over one thousand silver seekers—miners, businessmen, and families who began the settlement living in tents and log cabins. Rosita quickly developed into a classic western town with a general store, a blacksmith's, a schoolhouse, a small hotel, and of course, a rowdy saloon. But when the silver dried up, just a few years later, the prospectors and everyone else pulled up stakes and moved on.

When we arrived in Colorado, Rosita was a ghost town—with real ghosts. But that didn't stop Jeff and me from frequenting the old cemetery on a hill down the road. Wandering among the tipped and cracked headstones, peering at the faded inscriptions, we quickly forgot our life in Detroit. Our new playground was the ruin of Rosita—just a few splayed piles of gray wooden planks—and the abandoned mines. Traces of silver were said to be in the walls and ceilings of these holes in the hillside, an irresistible temptation for a couple of boys, just eleven and twelve. Thrilled by the prospect of danger and disobedience, we often took our flashlights and explored those old mines, crawling inside and making our way through a maze of unstable support timbers, deep into the pits, searching for silver.

"I must have been crazy," Pop said, breaking the silence. "Remember the work that went into building that cabin?"

"Tell me about it!"

"I'd load up the old Datsun pickup with tools and lumber. Then I'd chug up and over that long, steep mountain pass." Pop was wide awake now.

"How did you know how to build a house?" I asked.

"I *didn't* know!" he laughed. "But I figured it out. I made up the plans myself, and they were pretty rough. But in the end, it turned out perfectly."

It was perfect. A small, comfortable house in the style of a Swiss chalet, nestled in the trees with a view of the glowing Sangre de Cristo Mountains. It even had gingerbread trim and a wrap-around deck.

"Jeff and I helped a little," I said, laughing.

"That's right. I needed you to help me lift the walls when we framed it."

"Remember the adobe barbecue?" I said.

"What a big muddy mess that was," Pop laughed. "You and Jeff were determined to make your own sundried bricks out of clay from the backyard. I don't how you convinced me to haul all that straw and clay up that mountain."

"But it was you who made the molds for the bricks while we mixed it all up."

"I know, I know," he said. "Where'd you ever get an idea like that?"

"Probably from you!" I laughed.

The sun had set, and I reached for the switch on the table lamp.

"Do you remember the ghost?!" Pop almost shouted in the dark as he suddenly sat up in his chair, excited, his hands on his knees.

I remembered the ghost all right.

One morning, at the front edge of daybreak, I was in the loft of the cabin. Pop was brewing coffee in the kitchen below, and I lay awake in bed, eyes closed, perfectly relaxed, taking in the aroma. I was visualizing the sun's first rays illuminating the room through the big windows when, suddenly, I had the vague notion, a strong suspicion, that someone was watching me. I opened my eyes. A few feet above me, the torso of a translucent, green-glowing miner hovered in the air, staring down at me. The figure of the apparition was raggedly cut off at the waist, but I had no doubt he was a miner, judging by his filthy, tattered jacket and the worn look on his rough, bearded face. He was watching me with a friendly, reassuring look, gently smiling.

I was totally freaking out.

Paralyzed with fear, I tried in vain to scream. Our eyes locked, and after a moment, I began to calm down. For a moment we simply gazed at each other. Then, with a sudden flash, the apparition shot over the headboard of my bed and through the back wall, slicing through the brisk morning air toward the abandoned mines behind the cabin.

"But what really blew me away, " I said after a moment, "was that nobody at the breakfast table that morning doubted me or seemed the least bit surprised!"

"The place just had a certain magic, I think," Pop said.

We sat in the dark for a few more minutes.

"So, Pop," I said, switching on the lamp. "Where did *you* get the idea to build a family-sized cabin, mostly by yourself?"

"Well, I was driving errands around Pueblo, and I noticed this hardware store was having a going-out-of-business sale. I swung in, just out of curiosity," he said. "Out back they had a pallet stacked with these really nice, big windows. And they were practically giving them away! So I bought them and drove them home in the truck."

"And...," I prompted.

"Now I had all these windows," he grinned. "So I *had* to build a house to go with them."

That was classic Pop.

"You know, I never really understood," I said. "After all that, why in the world did you sell it?"

"I was sixty-nine," he began, "living out in the middle of nowhere. Your mother and I had to face facts. The nearest hospital was forty-five minutes away."

I nodded.

"Besides," he said. "I wanted to do something different!"

Always forward, never back. Pop was forever ready for the next thing.

For seventy-five years, a cardboard box of old documents, letters, clippings, and photographs went wherever my family went. Collected and preserved by Babcia, the memorabilia made the trip from Detroit to Pueblo. When my grandmother passed away, my mom became custodian of the box, putting items in Ziplock bags, occasionally adding new things, and attaching explanatory notes. She took it along to Rosita where it sat in a cabinet for ten years, and then it was carefully stored in a closet when my parents moved to Arizona. After my father passed away, my sisters found it and gave it to me. For the book, they said.

I dug right in, of course.

What first caught my eye were the cards home. Among the papers and photographs were just a few postcards written by my father while imprisoned at *Stalag Luft I*—four to be exact.

Kriegsgefangenenlager (Prisoner-of-war camp)
Postkarte
Datum: June 25, 1944
Stalag Luft I

Dear Hank,

I'm taking things pretty easy here; not much to do except get lazy! I haven't received any letters yet but hope to soon. You were wrong about that picture I sent home and Wanda was right. Having a wonderful time and wish you were here.

Love Barney

When I read my father's faded note to his brother-in-law, I couldn't believe just how brief and uninteresting it was, a parody of a picture postcard written while on holiday in the tropics. I wondered what my Uncle Hank had thought of it at the time.

Having a wonderful time and wish you were here.

Pop's notoriously dry wit made me laugh. He was known for his ironic sense of humor, and it was clear from his stories that for POWs, gallows humor was an indispensable coping mechanism. I recalled Pop's greeting when he arrived at the camp, his imprisoned comrades hamming up the suffering for a laugh. He had stated to me, repeatedly, that the worst parts about prison camp were the boredom and the hunger. As officers, the men were not forced to work, so in a twisted way, I suppose he *was* "taking things pretty easy" and "getting lazy." Knowing him, I can believe he wouldn't see any point in complaining, raising useless alarm, and worrying the family. And he would have anticipated that the German censors would black out any hint of the inhospitable conditions in the camps.

Scrutinizing the few words written on the card, I wondered what my father could have meant about *the picture*. What picture? Even if he had *had* a picture in his possession, he couldn't have sent it from the camp because prisoners were allowed to write only on postcards issued to them. And how could he have gotten an opinion on the picture from my Uncle Hank if he had not yet received any mail? Was it in reference to something he had sent months earlier from the base in England? To bring up such a thing in a brief note seemed cryptic, and the phrasing—*You were wrong... and Wanda was right*—Could it be a coded message? I had read somewhere that POWs often embedded clever code words and phrases in their letters home to conceal real information that the Germans would otherwise censor. But I would need a cryptanalyst—or another conversation with my father—to determine whether it really was code and what the code meant.

To my disappointment, the other postcards were even more dull, lacking even a hint of encryption:

Kriegsgefangenenlager (Prisoner-of-war camp)
Postkarte
Datum: Aug. 13, 1944
Stalag Luft I

Dear Sis,

I'm writing just to say that I'm all right and hope you are, too. As yet I haven't received any mail but am pretty sure I'll get one within the next month if you wrote soon enough. Give my love to Mom and take care of her for me.

Love— Barney

When the collection of memorabilia came into my hands, I found only four brief postcards from my father, but I have no doubt that these were all that his family ever received. Among them were the seven postcards from the *Short-Wave Amateur Monitors Club* and the telegrams and letters from the Army, so it seems like Babcia saved everything. The short note to my Aunt Wanda betrays a hint of melancholy as Pop once again mentions that he has not received any mail. I could scarcely imagine my father's loneliness and misery. And I wonder, how many letters in all those months did they all write that were never delivered?

One card, for no apparent reason, is the only one written in block letters instead of cursive. Although it has more of Pop's dry humor, it also hints at the realities of being a prisoner in the dark winter of Northern Germany: *Slow and cold.*

Kriegsgefangenenlager (Prisoner-of-war camp)
Postkarte
Datum: Nov. 16, 1944
Stalag Luft I

DEAR FOLKS,

EVERYTHING HERE IS SLOW AND COLD; BUT THANKS TO BOOK PARCELS WE HAVE PLENTY TO READ. I'M ONLY WRITING A CARD TODAY BECAUSE I HAVE A LOT OF SEWING AND DARNING TO DO. AND DON'T LAUGHT!! I'M PRETTY BAD BUT IT HOLDS TOGETHER FOR A WHILE.

Barney

The cryptanalyst in me is tempted to read meaning into every word. What does time spent mending have to do with writing a card? He says he is *pretty bad*. Ostensibly at sewing and darning. But could he be hinting at his health, physical and mental? *It holds together for a while.* Maybe it's too modern a way to look at it. Probably, it's too poetic for my father, and too armchair psychologist of me. I wish I had looked into this box of old documents before Pop passed so that I could ask him what, if anything, some of these notes meant. More questions that can never be answered.

Sorting through the letters and clippings from the folders in the old cardboard box, I came across a few pages of a newsletter called *The Marauder Thunder*, February 1993, likely published by the B-26 Marauder Historical Society. The pages contained numerous short articles on former B-26 crewmen, as well as a few pictures. An article high-lighted in faded yellow recounts a story by a former Royal Air Force Typhoon pilot named Seymour "Buck" Feldman. In 1981, Buck had met a former *Luftwaffe* FW-190 pilot in Munich. The two pilots became friends, exchanging gifts and photographs over the years. According to Buck, this pilot had twenty-one allied aircraft to his credit, including a Marauder on January 23, 1944. In 1992, the German ace visited Buck in Albuquerque, New Mexico, and told him this story:

FW-190 Pilot Tells of Shooting Down Marauder

I started with four FW-190s in Wevelgem at 15:07. Because of bad weather in the south, we climbed up to 8000 meters between Ghent and Lille. We attacked the Marauders from behind, 4 Spitfires crossed in at 5000 meters.

I had my 16ᵗʰ victory—the Marauder crashed quite near the channel at Gravelines. After shooting I dived with full power, but 2 Spitfires hunted me—they came nearer and nearer. Then I pulled my 190 into the sun and lost the Spitfires.

Oblat shot down another Marauder and a FW got a Spitfire. Our 3 victories were announced in the daily German WEHRMACHTS BERICHT. The time of the victory was at 15:35 on the 23ʳᵈ of January, 1944.

The editor of the newsletter then addresses the reader:

With the information given above there must be a reader who can identify the mission, the Group and/or the Crew. Let us hear from you.

Holy smokes! I thought. The account given by the German pilot hit me like a glass of cold water to the face. It was a reminder: There are billions of people in the world, every one of whom is the protagonist of their own story. During all the time I had listened to and recorded Pop's stories, it never occurred to me that there were also people *on the other side*, people with their own stories and complexities. It shocked me to think of this German ace claiming the hit on my father's B-26 as his "16ᵗʰ victory." Now, knowing that the "evil German" who shot down my father had become friends with a former RAF pilot, I had to think of him as a person, whose point of view and survival instinct were just as real as my father's.

It felt like another missed opportunity, another question I would like to have asked Pop. Would he have wanted to meet this pilot, the man who had almost killed him, who had doomed him to sixteen months in a POW camp, who had sentenced him to a lifetime of chronic pain? My father had received the newsletter in 1993, and I vaguely remembered his showing it to me back then. Clearly, he had not pursued further correspondence. But he kept the letter. All these years later, I had the idea of trying to contact the German pilot's family, but I'm not sure what I would have said to them. Maybe, like Buck, we would exchange a few gifts and photographs. Maybe it would be nice for us just to acknowledge that we're all human, each defending our one chance at being alive.

About those Spitfire pilots who hounded the German ace and drove him away from his prey. My father had often mentioned their importance to the Army's bombing missions. The Supermarine Spitfire Mark I had a 1,130-horsepower Merlin engine, a range of 500 miles, and eight machine guns that could deliver 160 rounds per second. Its state-of-the-art aluminum alloy frame and elliptical wings made it the most agile fighter in the sky. And it was designed to be adapted to different purposes. The Spitfires provided crucial air support for the D-Day landings, and many were modified as fighter-bombers to carry out attacks on German ground forces. These British planes were often piloted by exiled Polish airmen.

In 1939, the German-Soviet juggernaut vanquished the Second Polish Republic. Most of the military units, including the Polish Air Force, were evacuated to Romania and Hungary, after which, thousands made their way to France. In 1940, after the Nazis captured France, many of the Polish airmen retreated to the United Kingdom and joined the Royal Air Force.

Although the Polish pilots had mastered flying while defending Poland against Hitler and Stalin, the RAF brass initially doubted their usefulness—it seemed the *Luftwaffe* had easily defeated the Polish Air Force, and German propaganda constantly boasted about Poland's ineptitude. For months, the RAF denied the pilots their Polish independence and rank, requiring them to wait in English training camps. Meanwhile, the less-experienced RAF pilots were suffering heavy losses. Finally, in cooperation with the

Polish government-in-exile, the British government swallowed its pride and allowed for the creation of several Polish squadrons and a training center as part of the RAF. Once the squadrons were allowed to join the action, British authorities could not deny how effective the Polish airmen were.

My father had the privilege of meeting a few of these Polish Spitfire pilots.

"They landed at our base in Colchester," Pop told me, "and since I could speak Polish, my Commanding Officer asked me to escort them on a tour. They were part of a group of pilots that managed to escape from Poland before the Germans occupied the country. Then they fled to England and formed their own fighter group under British command."

The Polish airmen had a reputation: They were fearless, reckless even, and their high success rates made them the toast of London, even though the censors tried to keep it quiet.

"That must have been quite an honor to speak with them," I said.

"It certainly was," he said. "This Spitfire group escorted us on several of our bombing missions. Believe it or not, one of the first things they told me was how much they admired our bravery, flying through an anti-aircraft barrage to our target. They were referring to that last minute of the Schiphol bomb run."

"I believe it!" I said. "What did you say to that?"

"Well, I said how much I admired *them* because I had heard that the Polish fighter group always volunteered for the most dangerous missions."

"I wonder why," I said.

"I asked them about that," Pop said. "They answered that they did so because they had nothing to lose. They said Poland would never be free, no matter who won the war. If Germany won, it would belong to Germany; if the Allies won, Russia would claim Poland. One was just as bad as the other as far as they were concerned."

The pilots were sadly not mistaken about their fate. After Hitler lost the war, the Soviet Union commandeered the entire Polish territory. The ironically named "Polish People's Republic" ruled with terror, nationalized industry, and collectivized agriculture. Only a few of the airmen returned to Poland; the rest remained in Britain, exiled from their native country. Communist rule would not end until 1990. If Belgium is the battlefield of Europe, it seems Poland is the football, having been kicked around throughout the centuries. But that's another story.

"Anyway, I was happy to learn that my Polish was good enough to carry on a conversation with someone from Poland," Pop concluded in his inimitable, laconic way.

Once again, my father had told me a story that seemed simple enough, but upon reflection, had disturbing implications. It was only later that I contemplated the desperate situation these pilots were in, that all of Poland was in. To me, my Polish grandparents' generation had seemed rigid, stuck in their ways, forming close-knit neighborhoods, and keeping company with their own kind. But they were also immigrants, if not exiles. They had had the courage to leave their homeland behind in search of a better life. I wondered if my father's maverick audacity was an expression of an inherited trait, an ancestral characteristic, passed down through history and blood.

POP (RIGHT) SHAKING HANDS WITH A POLISH SPITFIRE PILOT

CHAPTER 13

Liberation

... never forget that until the day when God shall deign to reveal the future to man, all human wisdom is contained in these two words—Wait and Hope.

—Alexander Dumas
The Count of Monte Cristo

D Day: On June 6, 1944, the combined forces of the Allied armies delivered five naval assault divisions to the beaches of Normandy. Given the codename OVERLORD, the D-Day operation was the largest invasion force in history. Operation OVERLORD began the liberation of France, bringing much needed optimism to *Stalag Luft I* as the prisoners dared to hope that the war was finally coming to an end. There was still a long and uncertain future ahead of them, but at least they had reason to believe that eventually they would be liberated and returned home.

"It was just indescribable joy when we heard the news," Pop told me as we sat together on his porch at Silver Springs. "It gave us hope that maybe the war would soon be over."

But the Allied victory came at a price. Following the Normandy invasion, conditions at the camp deteriorated from boring and unpleasant to dire and desperate. The Nazis could see that the German army was losing the war, and by winter, their attitude toward the POWs had hardened.

The camp *Kommandant*, Colonel Oberst Scherer, had been in command at *Stalag Luft I* since October 1942. A zealous Nazi, he had always dealt harshly with the POWs, and as the Allies closed in, he became vengeful. He seemed to take pleasure in punishing an entire barrack for one man's disobedience. More and more, Scherer began sentencing POWs to solitary confinement for minor infractions. Not only did he confine prisoners for no good reason, but he also denied them their Red Cross foodstuffs and tobacco. And he issued vindictive new guidelines, authorizing guards to use firearms, to avenge what they saw as "insults to German honor." The German officers interpreted this order rather loosely, and prisoners were being shot at for little more than a dirty look or muttered obscenity.

Stalag Luft I was a huge camp with 9,000 prisoners. My father recalled a different kind of shift in the German soldiers' behavior: "The guards became friendlier," he said. "So we knew that they were accepting the fact that they were losing the war. They kept telling us that the Nazis were the ones who wanted the war, not them. I kind of doubted this, after seeing how the civilians acted when I was first captured. At the time, they seemed to believe Hitler's propaganda that they were the superior race and would control all of Europe. But maybe they were just afraid of appearing disloyal."

"Or being shot," I said.

Pop nodded grimly.

Whatever their motives, it seems at least some of the enlisted Germans wanted to make nice while the brass wanted to tighten its grip on power.

In December 1944, an American Colonel, Hubert Zemke, arrived at *Stalag Luft I* and immediately became the Senior Allied Officer (SAO). Known as one of the most distinguished World War II fighter commanders in the European theater, his 56th Fighter Group, the "Wolfpack," was credited with 665 air-to-air victories. Zemke himself had 17.75 confirmed victories in 154 combat missions, putting him in the top twenty-five of all Army Air Forces World War II fighter pilots. The Colonel had been captured after his P-51 broke up in bad weather, and he was forced to parachute into enemy territory. Little did the inmates of the camp realize that it was their lucky day, for it was Zemke who was responsible for the uniquely peaceable way *Stalag Luft I* was liberated. For one thing, his American parents were German immigrants, and his fluent German enabled him to communicate effectively with the camp officials. He could also speak Russian and was a superb negotiator, having worked at the U.S. Embassy in Moscow.

In January 1945, not long after Colonel Zemke took command of the POWs, *Kommandant* Scherer was suddenly transferred, and Oberst von Warnstedt took over, carrying on with Scherer's draconian policies, perhaps even more viciously. Food supplies were further reduced as deliveries of German rations began arriving later and later. Von Warnstedt callously held back supplies and limited the amount of food a prisoner could save from his Red Cross parcel. Starvation became the new reality, the men were being terrorized, and it was hard to keep the faith.

"We all looked like skeletons," my father told me. "My weight dropped from about 160 to 110 pounds."

But the war in Europe was undeniably nearing its end, and it was a desperate time for Hitler's army. The war was over for Germany, the Allies were closing in, and those in charge were looking out for themselves. Worse, the Russians were coming. As my father explained, "The Russian strategy was to strike terror in the hearts of people in their path. It worked very well because practically everyone fled before their arrival and headed for the American front lines. Being captured by the Americans scared them a lot less than facing the Russians!"

As a result, most of the POW camps throughout the eastern sections of German territory would begin evacuating in January of 1945. Terrified of the Red Army, the Germans decided it was time to retreat, and they made plans to march thousands of ill-equipped prisoners hundreds of miles to escape the Russians.

As the harsh winter lingered on into the new year, the German rations continued to dwindle, and the Red Cross parcels dispatched from Switzerland went missing. This is when some of the men became too weak to get out of bed. Despite the severe treatment of the POWs under von Warnstedt, in conversation, SAO Zemke sensed that the *Kommandant* was disillusioned, and that he might be reasonable. Both men knew that the Allies were launching an offensive and entering Germany.

"Sometime after World War I, the major countries of the world held what was called the 'Geneva Conventions,'" Pop reminded me. "They put together what they considered humane ways to conduct a war, or at least as humane as possible."

The Geneva Conventions having established international legal standards for humanitarian treatment in war, the Germans must have known that they could be prosecuted for war crimes if they lost the war.

"Our planes had been dropping leaflets," my father told me, "warning the Germans that they would be held accountable for the safety of prisoners of war."

Once Hitler lost control, the Germans would be at the mercy of the Allies. Soon it would be every man for himself.

Starting in January and February 1945, prison camps throughout the eastern German-held territory were evacuating personnel as well as POWs. Following the German strategy of staying ahead of the Red Army, the Germans forced prisoners to march hundreds of miles in sub-zero weather, without shelter, without proper clothing, and without sufficient food. Many of these famished POW refugees marched right into *Stalag Luft I*, which was already overcrowded and desperate for rations.

Camp morale hit rock-bottom. In late March, SAO Zemke persuaded *Kommandant* von Warnstedt that they could alleviate the food shortage for both prisoners and German soldiers by allowing POWs to drive, under German guard, to the nearby port in Lubeck to pick up the Red Cross parcels before they could be pilfered. Knowing that the Swiss Protecting Power representative would be visiting *Stalag Luft I* in April, von Warnstedt agreed. The parcels were a huge relief to all concerned, and Zemke was establishing a collegial relationship with German officials.

In the April 14, 1945, edition of the *POW WOW*, the prisoners learned that the American General George S. Patton's Third Army was advancing in the West. The Russians had taken Vienna; they were approaching Germany from the East. The weary prisoners were hungrier than ever, but because the Allies were on their way, the monotony of the camp was transformed into intense anticipation. Everyone knew that this nightmare was almost over, but of course no one knew how the ordeal would end. As the POWs followed the advances of the Allies, they quietly speculated about their fates: Which front would reach them first?

"We soon realized that the Russians would be the ones to liberate us," Pop recalled.

"How did you know?" I said.

"We could hear them coming!"

By late April, the sounds of cannon fire could be heard booming in the distance—the Russians were advancing toward the camp from the east. As the fighting moved ever closer to Barth, SAO Zemke had continued using his language skills, the Red Cross parcels, and a little bit of subterfuge to gain respect and influence among the Germans, and as the Russian artillery came closer, he assured von Warnstedt that the *Luftwaffe* would be treated humanely once the Allies gained control.

Toward the end of April, von Warnstedt informed Zemke that he had orders to move the camp to prevent it from falling into the hands of the Red Army. Everyone—all German personnel and all prisoners—would have to evacuate *Stalag Luft I* within twenty-four hours. The order to evacuate the camp had apparently come from Hitler himself, via Heinrich Himmler. They were to walk 150 miles, and Zemke knew that his men, in their weakened condition, could not go the distance.

"Our Commander called the *Kommandant's* bluff," Pop told me.

"That was a bold move," I said.

"Yes and no. He realized that if we refused to go, then the Germans would have to use force. This meant that 200 German soldiers would have to shoot all 9,000 prisoners!"

The gamble worked: Zemke wouldn't budge, Von Warnstedt did nothing, and bloodshed was averted. And so the prisoners went on waiting for the Russians.

And then, one morning, the prisoners awoke to the eerie sound of silence.

"We were not awakened for the usual roll call, and everything was quiet," my father recalled, still amazed. "As I stepped outside, I noticed that all the guard towers were empty—no guards were in sight anywhere!"

While the prisoners slept, their captors had deserted the camp. A hand-sewn Stars and Stripes replaced the swastika on the flagpole.

"Everyone was gone!" Pop repeated, still dumbfounded. "They just ran out in the middle of the night, leaving everything behind—papers, file cabinets, orders, everything!"

Once they had opened the gates and made sure that the German compound was empty, my father and a few others broke into the locked offices of the *Kommandant* and rifled through the file cabinets.

"One of the documents we discovered, issued by Adolph Hitler himself, was a recent official order to *execute all prisoners immediately*," Pop told me. "The Germans were so terrified of the Russians, and of becoming war criminals, that the *Kommandant* had decided to ignore the Nazi high command and leave the camp under cover of darkness!"

On a lighter note, my father found his own official prison file and took home his photograph as a souvenir.

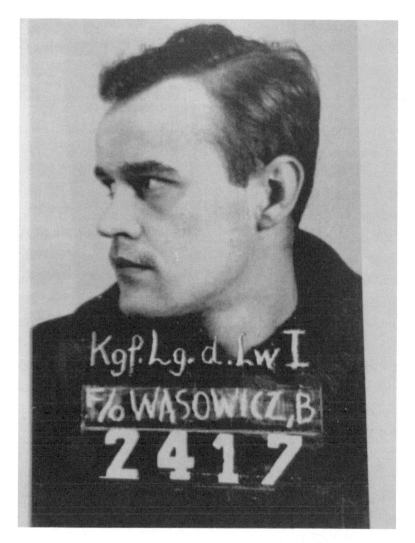

POP'S STALAG LUFT I PRISON PHOTOGRAPH

Unlike the rest of the 9,000 POWs at *Stalag Luft I*, SAO Zemke not only had known of von Warnstedt's plan to leave the camp, but in fact had brokered the deal. It was clear to Zemke that the German guards, mostly older men who had ordinary lives and didn't want to be there in the first place, would refuse to engage in a wholesale slaughter of POWs. Besides, anyone could see that the Nazis' reign of terror was waning; nobody wanted to add senseless war crime charges to what remained of their lives. After Zemke refused to put the POWs on the road, von Warnstedt tried a different tack. According to one account, on the morning of April 30, von Warnstedt asked Zemke to assume command of the POWs and allow all German personnel to leave the camp. The Russians were advancing rapidly from the east, and von Warnstedt desperately wanted to escape them. One way or another, the two commanders determined that the *Kommandant* would disregard orders from the Nazi high command and flee with his staff, leaving Zemke in charge of the camp. The two men agreed that the Germans would leave at midnight that night and head towards the American line to surrender. Supposedly, they shook hands on it, a gentlemen's agreement.

"Sounds like a big surprise party," I commented. "Why did Zemke not inform all the POWs that they were about to be liberated?"

"To keep us from starting a ruckus and attacking the guards!" Pop said, laughing. "Zemke was smart. He kept the deal quiet because he knew the POWs would retaliate. We later learned that at 23:50, Zemke and his staff said '*Auf Wiedersehen*' to the assembled Germans as they marched away from *Stalag Luft I*."

Once all German personnel had gone, Colonel Zemke officially took command of the camp.

"We had the entire camp to ourselves for a day, and further investigation revealed that most of the people in the town of Barth were also gone," my father informed me. "On the second day, we found out why. The Russians really were coming!"

Not the regular Russian Army, but the notorious *Red Army*.

"We called them the 'Terror Troops,'" Pop told me. "And, boy, were they brutal. They reminded me of the stories I'd read about Genghis Khan!"

The Soviet strategy was to send a rag-tag band of mercenary peasants to wreak havoc on towns and cities in advance of the regular army. These Russian patrols had little training and almost no equipment. But they more than made up for it in utter savagery.

The Russian patrols arrived May 1, the day after the Germans left. My father described the scene: "Heading our way came this horde of mostly Mongolians in horse-drawn wagons, officers on horseback, for as far down the road as the eye could see. I didn't see a single car or truck—not one motorized vehicle was in sight! They were dressed in all sorts of strange uniforms and brought plenty of women and cases of liquor right along with them."

Predictably, chaos ensued.

"Our commanders tried to keep us in the camp until arrangements could be made to fly us out," Pop explained. "They didn't want us scattered all over Germany."

Anticipating the potential for unruliness, Colonel Zemke had organized a select group of former POWs to act as military police, calling them the "Field Force," to keep the camp in order. After Zemke assumed command of the camp, these military police wore "FF" armbands and manned the guard towers, trying to keep the men tractable and in the camp. I smiled at the irony of the liberated POWs being held in check by other liberated POWs. Not to mention the futility. Of course, many of the POWs bridled at the idea of being "guarded" by their fellow inmates. Zemke tried to explain that it was for their own protection—there was still a war going on. They could not be wandering around on their own, unarmed and without proper uniforms or papers. They could be *shot!*

But the Russian patrol commander saw things differently. These men were *free*—his army had liberated them—and he wanted Colonel Zemke to have the barbed wire fences torn down immediately. At first Zemke refused, but was eventually compelled, possibly with a gun to his head, to order his men to take down the barbed wire. The energized men didn't have to be told twice, and with the help of the Russians, the fences came down within a couple of days.

Pop continued, "We later learned that these Russian troops—I use the word loosely—were allowed to rob, rape, steal, and do whatever they wanted to do as they advanced."

The Russian strategy worked. With the German soldiers out of the picture, and the people of Barth gone from their homes, the first order of business was to loot the shops and farms for food and everything else. Soon, the Russians had rounded up several hundred cows, herding them into the camp for the POWs to slaughter and eat.

"The Russians scoured the surrounding farms and confiscated everything," Pop told me. "It was like an invasion of locusts. In the camp, we had men who knew how to bake, so they took over the bakery in town, butchers to slaughter cattle, and so on."

As more Russians arrived the next day, Colonel Zemke lost control of the situation. The city of Barth became a scene of debauchery as the Russian "troops" paraded through the streets, drinking, collecting souvenirs, and harassing the few locals remaining in the town. Naturally, many of the liberated POWs wasted no time joining the revelry. After months or even years of captivity, nothing could stop them—not the risk of being shot, not the pleas of Zemke, and certainly not the threat of Zemke's MPs. My father, for one, "escaped" the confines of the camp as soon as he could.

"The first night after the Russians arrived, I found a way to sneak into town," Pop recalled with satisfaction.

"Really?" I said. "How did you manage that?"

"It wasn't difficult. Once it got dark, I and a buddy of mine quietly walked the perimeter, found an unguarded section of the camp, jumped the fence, and headed into town."

I laughed, shaking my head. Pop then described how, in the distance they saw flames and set out toward them like moths—their first walk abroad in sixteen months. They found the streets of Barth filled with spectacular bonfires and carousing Mongolians.

"This was something you would have to see to believe," Pop began. "They had several campfires set up in the middle of the street, concertinas playing, and dancing. It was one big party."

Confident that the robust Russians would not be alarmed by a couple of scrawny Allied POWs, Pop and his buddy walked right into the festivities.

"A few of the Russian dialects are close enough to Polish, so I could carry on a conversation with some of them," Pop told me. "They seemed happy to be able to talk to an American and offered me some of their brandy."

The looted livestock had already been butchered, and large chunks of meat sizzled on spits. There was singing and dancing and plenty of rotgut moonshine. This was pure bacchanalia. My father and his buddy were offered bad booze, cheap cigarettes, and steaming plates of roasted meat. They sneaked back into camp just before first light. In the morning, they both had hangovers of epic proportions, and they had never felt happier.

"You were lucky you got nothing worse than a hangover!" I said, laughing.

"It was kind of fun," he admitted. "But this all ended a couple of days later when the regular Russian Army arrived. They ordered the Red Army to move on to the next town and then restored some semblance of order in Barth. These soldiers were the direct opposite of the advance troops (I call them *troops* because I can't get myself to call them *soldiers*). The real Russians were dressed spick and span, and all orders were carried out on the run."

The "real" Russians may have been better dressed and organized, but the POWs remained in limbo. Although the Americans and the Russians were allies, it was clear that they were not necessarily friends. At this point, the United States was cultivating an uneasy alliance with Russia—in February, at the Yalta Conference, Stalin had agreed to join the Allies' fight against Japan once Germany had surrendered, and the war in Europe was over— nevertheless, the Russians remained distrustful of U.S. intentions. They seemed to think that, according to terms established at Yalta, American planes should not be allowed to fly over territory occupied by the Russians.

"Everything was strictly business with them," Pop continued. "They did not trust the Americans, and it took almost two weeks of negotiations with them before they allowed American B-17s to land at the nearby airport and fly us out."

The former prisoners became restless as the rumor mill fed anxieties about being used as pawns or taken to Siberia. Early on, the Russians pitched the idea of repatriating the men through the Russian Black Sea Port of Odessa, 1,500 miles away. Outraged, Colonel Zemke once again worked his wily magic, and on May 12, the 8th Air Force flew into Barth Airdrome and began a massive airlift called "Operation Revival." Even then the pace was agonizingly slow as the Russians allowed only one American aircraft on the field at a time.

"The last thing the Russians wanted was to have an entire fleet of U.S. bombers flying over their army and their hard-won territory," Pop said proudly.

✈ ✈
✈ ✈
✈ ✈

Kriegsgefangenenlager (Prisoner-of-war camp)
Postkarte
Datum: APRIL 8, 1945

Dear Mom,

The Russians are here and I am now free. I am all right and will be home soon. Put the duck in the oven and start baking because I'm really going to eat. Give my love to everyone; so long for a while.

Barney

The date on this card seems to be about one month earlier than the postmark date, which is May 12, 1945, so I wonder if my father had been holding on to it, waiting to be certain that he was leaving the camp. Or maybe he was delirious. Instead of the Prisoner-of-war-mail postmark from Germany, this card has a U.S. Army Postal Service postmark. In the upper right-hand corner, Pop had vigorously crossed out the word *Kriegsgefangenenpost* (Prisoner-of-war mail) and written the words *FREE (PLEASE RUSH)*.

LAST POW POSTCARD FROM POP

On May 15, 1945, my father walked out through the open gates of *Stalag Luft I* and boarded a B-17.

CHAPTER 14

In Bruges

Not what we have, but what we enjoy, constitutes our abundance.

—Epicurus

"Put the duck in the oven," he had written on his last postcard from *Stalag Luft I*. My father's deep appreciation of food was something I had always admired and taken to heart. This did not mean that he required pricey gourmet food, just good, basic, well-prepared food. And it had better be hot. It was funny to hear him say that, during the war, even before being in prison camp, he and his comrades had talked of little else. In my family, it was kind of the same. Not because we didn't have enough food to eat, but because we enjoyed the anticipation. As we were eating breakfast, we would be talking about lunch; at lunch we'd be talking about dinner, an endless cycle. Pop must have laughed and rolled his eyes every time his two athletic teenage boys would burst into the house raving that they were "starving."

I have very few vivid memories of my childhood. I can barely remember the house in Detroit where I grew up, the schools I attended, or the names of my large extended family. So it is no wonder that I really cannot say where I found my passion for growing, buying, cooking, and eating food. My father

173

certainly enjoyed and appreciated food—my whole family did—but not in quite the same way that I did.

From the moment I could hold a fork, I was obsessed with food, especially exotic foods, and I would seek out new flavors wherever I could find them. A box of tea from Ceylon, a fast-food taco, a La Choy Chinese Food kit—I found wonder in them all. To me, trying new cuisines is the best part of traveling. I revel in foreign food cultures; I will try anything, and if it is well prepared, I will usually like it. Sushi, raw cheeses, durian fruit ice cream, impala liver, street foods of all kinds—heck, even rutabagas—you name it, I've tasted it.

I especially love going to restaurants, and I relish the low end as much as the high. My mom was a great cook, and our working-class family of seven had little disposable income, so we rarely went to restaurants. On those rare occasions, nothing thrilled me more than being handed a menu though it wasn't as if I had a real choice. As my siblings could all attest, whether it was pizza or fine dining, we always knew, going in, that we were duty-bound to order among the cheapest items on the menu. Knowing this, I would choose quickly and then spend the extra time studying the lavish descriptions of the more expensive dishes. Even as a little boy, the idea that I might someday have my own money to spend on restaurant food enthralled me even more than the prospect of having my own car to drive.

It must have been during one of those infrequent outings, perusing an extra fancy menu, that I somehow encountered "Lobster Thermador" ostentatiously listed at the bottom of the page, priceless. I can only imagine where I could have come across this luxurious menu item since we went almost exclusively to family-friendly places for hamburgers, fried chicken or fish and chips. But somewhere along the way, Lobster Thermador appeared, and I knew, as a matter of course, that I would not be ordering it. It was *lobster* after all, the holy grail of fancy food, by far the most expensive dish on any menu. I couldn't quite grasp what the *Thermador* part was, but I didn't care—with a name like that, and a price like that, it simply *had* to be the most amazing dish on the planet. Thus began a lifelong, semi-serious refrain. Ask me, "What would you like for dinner?" and every time I'll answer, "Lobster Thermador!"

It had been less than a year since my mom left us some "mad money" to spend on anything we liked. Lo and I were not used to having extra money, and we resisted spending it, but it was Mom's dying wish that we enjoy ourselves a little, and now, thanks to her, we were in Bruges, Belgium.

World War II and my father's role in it were about the furthest things from my mind when Lo and I had chosen the Netherlands and Belgium for our Mom-sponsored vacation. Just as I never expected to order Lobster Thermador at a restaurant, I never really expected to find myself in Bruges. It was a fantasy first inspired by a strange film with ravishing cinematography. An aspiring Irish hitman horribly botches his first job and is then sent to Bruges to wait for instructions. While he is unimpressed by his surroundings, his partner is entranced, announcing that it is the best-preserved medieval city anywhere in Europe. Unlike Amsterdam, Rotterdam, and Antwerp, Bruges had not been seriously damaged by bombings. Twice occupied by Germany during the World Wars, the city had also been twice liberated, emerging with its medieval architecture and romantic canals virtually intact. Sometimes called the Venice of the North, Bruges is so magical it doesn't seem real: Everywhere you turn there are gothic buildings along cobblestone streets, flowing canals, curving bridges, graceful swans, charming cafés, extravagant chocolatiers. *In Bruges* takes viewers on a tour of the town's exquisite fairytale beauty, emphasizing the enchanted sense that a miracle had saved it from the ravages of war. We watched the movie again and again, each time dreaming about when we would go there.

Back at the Antwerp train station, the dream had once again seemed impossible—a mysterious accident and fire had knocked us off course, and then we had missed our stop—but after the comedy of errors, we were finally in a taxi on our way to our canal-side hotel.

The taxi driver voices his admiration: "Oh, Van Cleef Hotel, very nice."

It *is*. Ancient home of storied nobility, freshly renovated and decorated with a taste for old Hollywood. Our room has photos of Bogart and Bacall, Marilyn Monroe, Bridget Bardot. Audrey Hepburn with Gregory Peck in *Roman Holiday*. Posh furnishings with a Danish Modern flair. Our host, Benjamin, greets us with sincere offers of personal recommendations, a tour of the hotel, and a very welcome glass of Champagne in the luxe lounge. He suggests a classic meal of mussels and *frites*, making us a reservation at a friendly bistro, a ten-minute walk from the Van Cleef.

The bistro is cozy with a narrow tank of bright red tropical fish that serves as a panel between the tables. The mussels are fresh, the fries are crispy, the waiter is friendly.... It has been a very long day.

We awaken to sunlight streaming in through French doors after a night of unbroken rest in our king-sized bed, excited to begin exploring the museum city of Bruges. We find another comfortable café for lattes and croissants, bonus disk of dark chocolate included. A walking tour designed by travel guru Rick Steves leads us to the Belfry of Bruges where we climb a narrow, steep staircase of 366 steps, thinking of Alfred Hitchcock's *Vertigo* all the way. Thick ropes, oily with the countless hands that have clung nervously to them, help us up the long, winding steps. The view.... Incomparable.

We continue on, taking in the ancient churches, alleyways, cobblestones— all transporting us back to the Middle Ages, despite the circus atmosphere of vendors hawking waffles, fries, and chocolates. We find, with no trouble, a nice sidewalk café—so many to choose from—near the market square. The white asparagus is a culinary revelation. Prawns in diablo sauce, a dish of olives, a chilled glass of rosé for Lo, a local Belgian beer for me. It's sunny and warm out on the patio, perfect for people watching. Afterward, we walk, window-shopping as we go, back to the Van Cleef for a nap before dinner.

In the evening, finding the Italian restaurant recommended by Concierge Benjamin closed, we step randomly into Dan Huzzar, a comfortable Old-World restaurant that looks as if it's been serving *le souper* since the beginning of restaurant history. Right away, I notice a bubbling tank in the corner with a dozen or so lobsters in it, crawling about, their pinchers banded. The waiter leads us to a snug table by a window, and we order apéritifs as he hands us our menus. We sit for a moment, looking out the window, absorbing the splendor of it all. I open the menu. And there it is, at the very bottom, where it always is: *Lobster Thermador, MP* (priceless!). Lo notices it at the same moment. She looks up to see a certain look in my eyes, a gleam.

"Is it time?" she says with a smile.

"It's time," I say. "We're *in Bruges*—on Mother's Day no less—and it's high time we had some Lobster Thermador."

But first, Champagne.

"To Mom," I say, "who always said, at such times, 'Isn't this nice?'"

As we piece on Flemish white asparagus, my new favorite vegetable, the proprietor approaches our table with a mischievous look on his face. Then he waves a live claw-clicking lobster at us. "It is battery-operated!" he says with a grin.

"We'll take it!" I say, laughing.

And finally, we feast on Lobster Thermador. How was it? As my father would say, "This is a case of *If you hadn't been there, done that, you wouldn't be able to really comprehend it.*"

To conclude this benediction, the good-humored proprietor delivers an herbal digestif to our table, on the house.

Strolling around the magical city of Bruges that evening, holding hands with my wife, gazing at the old buildings, minding the cobblestones, crossing the canals—life couldn't get much better.

"Solitary confinement must have been absolute hell," I once commented to my father.

"Not really," Pop said. "It wasn't much different than any other day in the camp. You have to understand that we were already badly traumatized, starting with being shot down, injured, captured, and interrogated. We were used to being cold and hungry. And bored and brutalized. That's all we knew for months and months."

"But it must have been *awful*. I can't imagine how—" I began when he cut me off.

"Of course, you can't," he said, in an unusually serious tone.

I put down my pen and looked at my father. I had the feeling that he was about to tell me something he had wanted to say for a long time.

"You and your generation had it lucky," he continued. "Everything was easy for you. You got to pick where you went to school, or if you even wanted to go. You could choose whatever job you wanted, and when you got bored you could switch jobs. You could travel on a whim, wherever you wanted. You could get whatever kind of food you wanted." His blind eyes stared directly into mine.

"You don't know what it's like to suffer."

I stared back in stunned silence at what felt like an accusation. My gut reaction was to defend myself, to stand up for my generation. After all, it wasn't all easy for me. I'd had my ups and downs like anyone else. I'd worked hard. I'd sometimes struggled to lead a meaningful life. Pop seemed to be waiting for me to argue with him. And I could have argued the finer points. But considering what he had been through, what he had endured, I couldn't really claim to have known suffering, not as he had.

"You're right," I agreed.

"I am?" he said, a little taken aback.

"Absolutely," I said truthfully. I had never been one to argue with my parents, not because I always agreed with them, but because I don't like to argue, and I didn't see the point. Now, I found myself nodding in sincere agreement with my father.

"It's true," I said. "You and Mom had to grow up during the Depression. You both lost one of your parents when you were young. And then the war came along, and everyone had to make sacrifices. You went to war, got shot down, and spent sixteen months in a filthy, freezing POW camp with nothing decent to eat. And when you got back, everyone expected you to go on as if nothing had happened. Pick up the pieces and try to build a normal life. That couldn't have been easy."

He continued staring at me, as if he were waiting for the punchline. I went on.

"You and Mom raised five kids on what you called 'minor jobs.' You decided to leave Detroit and move the family out west, and you never looked back. None of us did! You may think that you never had an important job, or that you never 'made your mark,' but from where I'm sitting, you have accomplished a lot more than most people."

I paused.

"It's because of *you* that I never suffered, that I had it easy," I concluded. "You *made* it easy for me!"

"What do you mean?" he asked warily, still waiting for an argument.

"Remember when I decided to 'throw away' my career in biology, so Lo and I could travel for a few months? And then I did a menial job as a water-meter reader for two years even though I had two college degrees?"

"Yes."

"Remember when Lo and I decided to move to California, with no jobs waiting for us? And then I started at the bottom, working as a cellar rat in the wine industry even though I had two college degrees?"

"Yes."

"Do you remember what you said? You told me about *your* California dream when you were young. You said that you admired our courage to go and find whatever it was we were looking for."

"I said that?"

"You did. And it meant so much to me. It made me feel confident in my decision. It was refreshing to see your hidden 'throw-caution-to-the-wind rebel side,' too. You're always so practical and conservative. And so am I, most of the time. But I have an adventurous side. Just like you."

He shook his head, but didn't argue.

On that beautiful, memorable evening in Bruges, made possible by both my parents, I thought of my father and what he had been through. Like Antwerp, he had been captured by the Nazis, starved, brutalized, and robbed of a year and a half of his life. I was more like Bruges; I was aware of the deprivations and inhumanity of war, but I did not endure them firsthand. My life had not been ravaged by them. Like Antwerp, my father was liberated—he survived, rebuilt, and thrived. And like Bruges, I was very, very lucky that I had been protected.

CHAPTER 15

Camp Lucky Strike

My grandpa died before I was born, so, no interviews per se and according to his kids, he didn't talk too much about the whole experience.

—Bob Esser
Grandson of Robert (Bob) Carpenter

"We lined up, twenty to a group, boarded the planes, and took off for a cigarette camp in France," my father told me.

It was the last day of my visit, and we were sitting outside in the sunny courtyard of Silver Springs.

"Really?" I said shaking my head. "*Cigarette* camp?!"

"Sure," he said, laughing. "'Camp Lucky Strike,' to be specific. It was a holding camp set up to process the ex-POWs and arrange for our transport back to the States. I was there for two months. And yes, we got free cigarettes."

"Why did it take so long?" I wondered.

"There was no way they were going to send us stateside right away. We all looked so thin and haggard. It would have been too shocking for the folks at home. The Army wanted to fatten us up and check us out physically first."

Under "Operation Revival," the 8th Air Force swooped into Barth, one plane at a time, and evacuated the inmates of *Stalag Luft I*. While the Royal

181

Air Force soldiers were flown directly back to England, the Americans had a much longer journey ahead of them, so they were taken to a staging camp, where they prepared and waited to cross the Atlantic and return to the States.

So it was back to camp for the RAMPS—the former POWs were now called RAMPS—Recovered American Military Personnel. But this time it was to "Cigarette Camp." As France was freed, and liberation of Allied soldiers commenced, American forces quickly constructed more than twenty repatriation camps around the liberated ports of France.

"Why did they call them *cigarette camps?*" I asked.

"For security reasons," Pop explained. "They were code-named after the well-known tobacco brands back home. Referring to the camps without revealing geographical information helped ensure the enemy could not determine our precise location. The spies listening in on radio traffic would think that the topic being discussed was simply tobacco."

There was also a psychological premise for the names, I later learned. Cigarettes were comforting, especially popular American brands such as *Phillip Morris, Pall Mall, Old Gold,* and of course *Lucky Strike.* Soldiers, the commanders reasoned, wouldn't mind staying at a place where good cigarettes would be free and plentiful.

Lucky Strike happened to be the largest of the cigarette camps, with a capacity of 58,000 troops, packed onto a field just over two square miles. Located forty-five miles from the demolished port of Le Havre, the former staging camp for replacement personnel became an improvised city for American troops waiting to embark on the voyage home. Camp Lucky Strike was known as either "seventh heaven" or "complete chaos." For some, it was both. As my father would say, "If you hadn't been there, done that, you wouldn't be able to really comprehend it."

While this massive tent city on the coast of France was a big improvement over *Stalag Luft I*, Camp Lucky Strike was no day at the beach.

"It was lucky for us that we were there in early summer," Pop told me. "We sheltered in makeshift tents that would have been even more damp and drafty than the barracks in the prison camp."

During the first several days in the camp, spirits were high as the RAMPs absorbed the fact that they were free men again. They were kept busy with showers, delousing, new uniforms, and medical exams.

"The medical exam they gave us was a joke," my father informed me.

"How so?" I asked, a little surprised.

"Oh, they did the best they could, I guess, under the circumstances. But with that many men in such bad shape, the doctors had to focus on the ones who were too weak to travel or had infections or injuries and had to be hospitalized."

During eighteen months of evacuations, over 73,000 men would pass through this one staging ground, and there were the countless forms and applications to be filled out.

"Intelligence officers debriefed us about our last mission before being captured, our group, our target, and so on."

"One more interrogation!" I said.

"That's right," Pop said, laughing. "They also collected intelligence about how the Germans had treated us. And there were questions about crew members still missing in action," he said, looking down.

The scale of this mountain of paperwork must have been staggering. But at least it gave the men something to do.

Soon the exhilaration of liberation from prison camp and delivery to cigarette camp faded, and a dull waiting game began. Morale was a mixed bag of hope and impatience. The rule sent down by the War Department said that all American POWs who had been imprisoned for more than sixty days would be returned to the United States rather than returned to their units. But there was still the war against the Japanese to be won, and rumors circulated saying that some soldiers would be sent to the Pacific theater. These rumors added to the anxiety of those waiting to get back to their families and get on with their lives.

At Lucky Strike, it was unclear who, if anyone, was in charge; straight answers were in short supply. Unlike the order and discipline the men had been used to, first as soldiers and then as prisoners, it was disorienting to be untethered, with no direction and nothing to do but wait. This uncertainty was a different kind of torment. Although the men had been cleaned up and issued new uniforms which restored their dignity, they no longer had a mission or a purpose—"all dressed up with no place to go," as Pop put it. As soldiers, they followed the orders of their commanders; as prisoners, they tried to escape, obtain more food, or just survive; as inmates of cigarette camp, it seemed, they had only one job, and that was to gain weight.

We were all starved and in terrible condition," my father recalled. "I weighed in at 110 pounds. If the people at home could have seen us, they would be horrified."

But it wasn't a simple matter of consuming more calories. In this case, the men's eyes were indeed bigger than their stomachs, a condition that could be hazardous to their health.

In addition to the presumably sensible meals provided in the mess halls, the American Red Cross had set up a café and doughnut line, "Java Junction," where RAMPs could relax and socialize. The medical staff sternly advised the men to limit themselves to one doughnut, anticipating the assault on the weakened digestive systems of the emaciated soldiers.

"Some of the men couldn't control themselves," Pop recalled. "Some had to be hospitalized after gorging themselves on the doughnuts."

I tried to imagine a giant tent with hundreds of gaunt servicemen, lounging around smoking cigarettes, drinking coffee, and eating doughnuts. It's a wonder that any of them survived Camp Lucky Strike.

"I thought cigarettes were supposed to keep your weight *down*," I said. "Didn't Mom complain about gaining weight back when the two of you decided to quit smoking?"

Pop laughed. "'Reach for a cigarette instead of a fattening snack!' the ads used to say. It was kind of ironic."

While my father had become shockingly thin, many of the RAMPs arrived at cigarette camp dangerously malnourished, or even ill. After months or even years of subsisting on rutabaga broth, *Ersatzbrot*, powdered milk, a bite or two of horsemeat now and then, and cigarettes, adjusting to regular meals was difficult psychologically as well as physically.

"We couldn't eat very much at a meal, probably because our stomachs had shrunk," Pop explained. "So they fed us four times a day."

"What did you have to eat?" I asked.

"Creamed chicken and eggnog," Pop informed me. "Apparently, chicken was the easiest protein to digest."

"Okay, what else?" I asked.

"Creamed chicken and eggnog. I remember having creamed chicken and eggnog, over and over. Four times a day, every day, for two months. I guess they added some other foods eventually, but I just remember creamed chicken and eggnog."

I was about to say, "That sounds horrible," but I didn't want to have another discussion on how little I knew about suffering.

"I guess it beats ersatz and rutabaga broth," I said instead.

"Yes, I guess it was alright. They were trying to revitalize our digestive systems and fatten us up so that we would look halfway decent when we got home."

The medical staff attempted to control the men's diets, giving talks on digestion, and placing educational posters in the mess halls. They tried to explain that the men's stomachs and intestines, weakened by disuse, would need to be rehabilitated, that it would take time. For some of the former POWs, it would be years before their digestive systems could handle the foods they had been used to eating before the war. In the meantime, the men who could not control themselves suffered the consequences.

In between meals and hasty trips to the latrine, there was the monotony. Plenty of time with nothing to do. Once again, as in his post-liberation days at *Stalag Luft I*, my father was a captive of his own allies. In theory, authorization was strictly required for personnel to leave the camp. In fact, many RAMPs slipped through the gates and ditched the camp as they had longed to do while prisoners. According to one account, as many as 5,000 officers went absent without leave from Lucky Strike alone. So it should have been no surprise to me that, once again, true to form, my father also went AWOL.

One hundred miles from Le Havre, France, Paris was the usual destination for personnel leaves, authorized or not. The City of Lights beckoned the RAMPs, and American hitchhikers were a common sight on the road to Paris. Meanwhile, my father found himself traveling in style to Brussels. A few weeks before his release from Lucky Strike, he could not believe his eyes when he saw a B-26 landing on the adjacent field. Pop immediately jogged over to reunite with his former airplane. Even more incredible, he was astonished to find that the pilot was a good friend from his Bomb Group, the 386th. The pilot had stopped to refuel before heading to Brussels for a couple of days.

"Why don't you come along?" he said. Game for anything, Pop climbed aboard without a second thought.

By now I should have known better than to be surprised, but I had to ask, "Um, you went *AWOL?*"

Pop chuckled. "No one really expected us to stay in the camp," he said. "There was nothing else for us to do. They couldn't contain us. So a lot of us just slipped out whenever we had the chance."

Upon landing at the military base in Brussels, my father's lucky streak continued. At Lucky Strike, the rumor mill had been grinding out a story saying that some of the RAMPs would not be paid for their time, or they would be sent to the Pacific Theater of Operations to help make up for the months they had been rotting in prison camp. So Pop went to the payroll office to see if he had any money coming. He did. Apparently disregarding the fact that this officer was AWOL, a friendly clerk informed him that he was owed money for all the time he had spent in service at the prison camp. Then he counted out a cash advance of two hundred dollars, into Pop's hands. The clerk then called for a Jeep and a driver, and while they were waiting, he pulled out a bottle of Scotch and a bottle of gin from his desk and handed them to my father.

"Go have some fun!" he said cheerfully. I can only assume that Pop and his buddy did just that because he hardly remembered a thing about the third of his great escapes.

"Oh, nightclubs, I guess," Pop said absently. I didn't press for details on what must have been a wild and well-deserved night on the town.

"Really, the only thing I remember vividly was this weird statue," he said suddenly. "I remember standing at a street corner around dawn and just staring at this statue of a little boy peeing into a basin. Strangest thing."

Chapter 16

The End of the Line

Nothing is permanent, except change.

—Buddha

"He's stopped eating and lost a lot of weight," my sister Sandy informed me when she picked me up at the airport. "He's not talking much, either."

Lo and I had just returned home from Europe, and I immediately jumped back on a plane to Arizona to visit my father. The last time I had seen him, Pop was no longer feeling or looking great, and I thought about cancelling our vacation. Of course, he wouldn't hear of it. And no one else held it against me either. While I was away, my brother and two sisters made sure that our father had everything he needed. I could take a break and not worry about whether Pop was taken care of. Just as I knew I could trust them to take up the slack, they knew they could trust me not to abuse the privilege. This family spirit of dedication and cooperation had been imparted to us by our parents.

Mom had often told me that the thing she and Pop were most proud of was the fact that their children were so close. On many occasions, Mom shared this observation after repeating the gossip of the day from her friends at the pool or church. Too often, the women reported that their children, who rarely called and never visited, were also at odds with their brothers and sisters. Siblings fought constantly. They argued over care decisions for their aging parents. They bickered over finances. They squabbled about what they expected to inherit. The stories shocked me, and yet I had heard similar tales from my own friends. But for me and my siblings, getting along had never been an issue. It was something we all seemed to aspire to naturally. Not that it was always easy. As kids, we'd had our conflicts, and as adults, we didn't always see eye-to-eye. We all lived in different cities, and sometimes it was too long between calls and visits. But once we made the effort to get on the phone or to the same city, we fell back into the easy rapport of close friends. It was that commitment to closeness that got us through the difficult times during each of our parents' decline.

"In all my years of doing this, I have honestly never seen a family come together and deal with an event like this so well," Mom's angelic hospice nurse told me one time after a challenging day. "Seriously, you guys get a ten out of ten!"

At the time, I thought the nurse was just being nice. That was her job. It was only after my parents had both passed away, when I reflected back on those times, that I realized the truth of what she said. In contrast to so many dysfunctional families, we had all pitched in to see that our parents were taken care of to the best of our ability, come what may. No matter where we lived, or what difficulties we had, we all participated in a constant rotation of calls, letters, gifts, and visits. Somehow, we accomplished this with little discussion and no formal organization. It was understood. Each of us had our strengths and weaknesses, and we relied on each other to step up when needed and to fill the gaps.

We were a team. Assembled during childhood and trained by my parents, we had lived together in small spaces, traveled together long distances, and been there for each other no matter what. It started on "Lollipop," the little fiberglass ski boat Pop built in our garage in Detroit. Not satisfied with the occasional weekend jaunt to a nearby lake, he and my mom—Lolli— routinely loaded up all five kids and set off on excursions into Canada, camping on pristine islands along the way, fishing for our dinner, and picking wild blueberries to mix into our pancakes.

I once asked Pop how in the world he decided to build that boat.

"It was pretty simple," he said. "I saw a picture of the boat in a magazine with an ad, selling plans to make it yourself."

"And...," I prompted.

"And that was that."

"That was what?"

"*Well*, I had never built a boat before," he smiled. "I built her because I had no idea of what I was doing."

Aboard Pop's boat, jammed together for long periods, our family of seven rationed food from a big cooler, took turns cooking on the camp stove, and slept practically on top of one another. It was no place for tantrums or laziness or selfishness.

And that's how my family became a functioning crew. Now, I recognized parallels to the B-26 and her crew.

My sister Sandy was like the Flight Engineer, who is responsible for operating and monitoring the hydraulic, pressurization, fuel, and electrical systems of the aircraft. She was the one who moved Pop from Phoenix to Tucson so that she would be nearby to tend to his day-to-day needs. She ran errands, organized appointments, opened the mail, and kept Pop on a healthy schedule of activities. She kept him in the air.

Sue was the Navigator/Radio Operator who is responsible for keeping the aircraft on course, reaching the target and then the home base. She kept Pop engaged in life with spirited phone calls, gift boxes of fun garage sale clothing, and stacks of plastic containers stuffed with Pop's favorite treats. Not only did she keep him on a positive course, but she also served as the hub of communication between us all, calling and texting constant updates to family and friends.

My brother Jeff filled the role of the Gunner, who is responsible for protecting the aircraft. Along with the emotional issues of dealing with a dying parent come the practical details, and Jeff was the most like our father, methodical, with a head for numbers. He had the patience and know-how for the financial and legal arrangements. He tied up the loose ends.

My mom, of course, had been Pop's irreplaceable Co-pilot.

The only crew member left for me to represent was the Bombardier, whose job was quite obvious—get the bombs on the target. But what, metaphorically, were the bombs, and what was the target? My father had told me that his most important and unfinished goal, his target, was to "leave his mark." It was astounding to me, this notion of his, that he had not done anything significant and lasting during his life. He would say that he had only done what he called "minor jobs," and that he "was able to get by." As if it were only status and money that counted as significant. My informal interrogations seemed to please him, and I hoped he grasped the significance of our conversations. I decided that perhaps my role, in the end, was simply to listen and record. I would do my best to help him leave his mark.

I found him sitting up in his hospice bed, where he now spent most of his time, and he immediately asked me about our trip to Europe. I showed him the picture of me in front of the *Mannequin Pis* of Brussels, describing it in detail and asking him if he remembered it since I knew he couldn't really see it. I told him the whole history of the little statue, and he tried to be interested and amused. But I could see he was tired, so I got right to it, pulling out my notebook. I was still hoping to learn the details of Pop's voyage home from the war.

Before leaving home for this visit, I had looked at a few written accounts and photos of life at Lucky Strike, trying to imagine what a confusing, complicated, and chaotic time it must have been. Thousands of enervated men, drinking coffee, smoking cigarettes, eating chicken and eggnog, watching movies, and going AWOL. Thousands of men waiting for their number to come up.

Deloused, debriefed, and slightly fattened up, wave after wave of POWs filled trucks and trains bound for the coast to wait, once again, for transport home. Moving millions of liberated American POWs across the Atlantic Ocean was an epic undertaking.

"After about two months of this conditioning and waiting, we were put on a Liberty Ship and sent home," my father said simply.

"What was that like?" I asked him, pen poised.

"Long. Kind of boring. Not like a Caribbean cruise or anything," he laughed weakly. "There isn't much to tell."

"Right," I said. "How did you get from New York to Detroit? By train?"

"Yes, I took a train. Babcia and Wanda and Hank were all there waiting at the station. What a greeting that was! And when I walked into the house, the air was filled with the smell of roast duck."

"Must have been pretty intense," I suggested.

"I suppose so," he said, apparently not interested in saying more. "I was on leave after that, until the war came to an end, and I got an honorable discharge. Then I hoped to pick up my life where I left off."

He seemed to have nothing more to say. I sat quietly for a few minutes, reading my notes.

"I wish I could think of some profound statement as an ending to my story," he said suddenly. After all this time, he still didn't see what I could see. I pondered what to say to encourage him. Then I remembered the newsletter with the account from the former *Luftwaffe* FW-190 pilot.

"Here's a question for you, Pop," I said. "The German pilot who shot you down—what if he walked into this room right now? What would you say to him?"

Pop thought about it for just a moment. His answer was as brief as it was surprising.

"I'd thank him."

I considered this, recalling a brief conversation we'd had a while back when Pop had described the implications. He told me that, had he not been shot down, he would likely have been part of the D-Day Invasion. That utterly devastating campaign would have been tough to get through alive.

"So, you realized that, even though prison camp was hell, you stood a very good chance of being killed if you were still flying?" I asked.

"No, it's not that. I mean, it's partly that, but it's a lot more."

Eyes closed, brow furrowed, he looked serious now, an expression I didn't often see in my father. I sat back and waited.

Reluctantly, he began, "The past few months I keep thinking about the squirrel. Do you remember the squirrel?"

"Um, what squirrel?"

"One time, after the war, I was in the woods with your Uncle Harry. We were shooting rifles, target practicing. Uncle Harry pointed at a tree in the distance. There was a small clump of branches near the top, looked like an old bird's nest. 'Shoot it!' he said. Well, I did, and we saw something fall out of the tree...." Pop turned his head toward me, blind eyes wide.

"I wanted to cry," he whispered. "Why would I do that? Why did I kill that squirrel? It was senseless. But I did it. Totally senseless."

He was agitated now. But he went on. Searching for the right words, he recounted a few facts about his beloved airplane. Although it turned out to be a great medium-range bomber, the B-26 was really designed for low-level attacks on enemy sites such as bridges, roads, artillery posts—and troops. Up until D-Day, all of Pop's missions had involved precision bombing, at relatively high altitude, of airport runways and V-1 and V-2 missile sites.

Certainly the bombs he dropped over eighteen missions had killed some German soldiers. But probably not too many. More importantly, from 12,000 feet, one cannot see the carnage and death below. But the Invasion required quite different tactics for B-26 pilots.

"I had control of four .50 caliber machine guns in the nose of the airplane, with four long strings of ammo that snaked all the way back toward the tail. In training, I practiced firing them all the time, at little targets in a field."

194

He swallowed back tears.

"I would have killed a lot of people. I would have flown in low, sometimes only fifteen feet off the ground, at high speed, and fired my guns into German troops. And I would see what I was doing. I would even be able to see their faces."

"And that's why you would thank the German pilot who shot down your airplane?" I said, moved to tears myself. "Because it meant that you didn't have to kill any more people?"

He nodded, covering his face with his hands.

✈ ✈
✈ ✈
✈ ✈

The last day of my visit, my father was the one asking the deep questions.

"Tony, why am I still here?"

He didn't need to explain. He had a condition the staff at Silver Springs called "geriatric failure to thrive." He no longer had his wife, his vision, or his health, so what was the point? He had few regrets. He had experienced so much. He had a loving family—children and grandchildren. But now he was mostly bedridden; he had nothing he could or even wanted to do. He was ready to go. His predicament reminded me strangely of the eighteen months he spent in prison camp and then cigarette camp, but this time, the only escape was death itself.

I moved my chair closer to his bed.

"Well, Pop, I can't say for sure, of course," I said. It was such a privilege to be sitting here with my father, my hero. His trust in me was almost overwhelming as he really seemed to be looking to me, his youngest son, for answers. I dug deep into my core beliefs, looking for simple words to comfort him.

"Listen," I began. "I believe that everything that comes to us in this life is exactly what we need it to be. Everything that happens is somehow for our own good. We may understand it, or we may not. Either way, I think that every moment must have some meaning and offer some sort of lesson. It's up to us to pay attention and learn what it is."

He was listening intently. He seemed to be thinking very carefully about what I was saying.

"Maybe there is more for you to learn before you go," I said finally.

The predawn ride to the airport was tough. The desert air felt heavy, humid, oppressive. Though Pop hadn't spoken of it, we both knew that this was the last time. I had said goodbye, knowing I would never see him again. Sitting on the airport shuttle, I felt lost in the dark. At the airport, everything looked lifeless and ugly under the florescent lighting. I sat staring at nothing. I wanted a coffee but decided, *Damn it, I'm not standing in line and paying that for a lousy Dunkin' Donuts coffee.* Pop would have approved and said that their coffee was poor quality and certainly not hot enough. Mom would have said it was too expensive. I had to agree. It was a little disconcerting how much I found myself agreeing with my parents lately. I glanced at the board. My flight was late. I had plenty of time but little motivation. I felt done in. I moved toward an isolated corner of the terminal and sat down, exhausted. But I pulled the notebook out of my backpack and started writing:

My last morning with Pop was typical of me—I waited until the last minute to pack before my flight, and I was gulping a cup of green tea while stuffing wadded t-shirts into my bag. My father was sitting up in bed, waiting for me to leave. Tension filled the small room.

"I had a nightmare last night," Pop blurted out.

I stopped packing. Whenever I had talked to him about dreams, he always insisted he never had them, or at least never remembered them. Now, he'd had not just a dream, but a *nightmare*. He needed to talk about it, and I was intensely curious, so I sat down in the chair by his bed and listened to him.

He relaxed his head back into the pillow and half closed his eyes. "I guess it wasn't really a nightmare. But it was so *weird*. I was walking inside of a big train station. I was going somewhere. I was the only one in there, but the hallways were all lined with marble statues of people."

A long pause followed.

"Who were the people?" I asked. "Did you recognize any of the statues?"

"Oh yes," he nodded. "They were all people I knew. Friends and neighbors and family. But as I walked through the station, they all started moving around. Like they were slowly starting to come to life. I wasn't scared or anything. It all seemed very peaceful. Then I woke up."

He waited for me to say something.

I'm not one who is easily impressed, but hearing Pop tell me about his dream was electrifying. Just before going to bed the night before, I had been leafing through the Hospice Information book, half buried in the piles of papers covering every flat surface in my father's apartment. As I flipped through it, what immediately caught my eye was a brief section titled "Confusing Conversations." According to this chapter, people who are close to death will often interject ordinary conversation with seemingly non-sensical thoughts and comments. Oftentimes, the person will speak of things related somehow to transportation. For example, "I'm going to get on the highway now" and "Look—The big bridge is over there." I had been thinking about "confusing conversations" as I drifted off to sleep.

Now I told him, "Pop, your dream... that's incredible!"

"It is?"

"It's more than incredible. It's what we talked about yesterday. It's part of your life lesson. You're getting prepared for your next mission. Those statues were of people who were stone dead to you. Now those people are coming back to life for you, to greet you, to go with you. You're not afraid anymore.

You're getting on that train to somewhere, and wherever it goes, Mom and Bill will be waiting."

He gazed at me but didn't say a word, his face totally blank. Then, after a few moments, he exhaled and lay still as his focus turned inward. Then he smiled—a smile completely at peace with the world.

CHAPTER 17

Follow Your Dreams

So it goes.

—Kurt Vonnegut
Slaughterhouse-Five

My father's memorial service was low-key, just as he had wanted. Unlike Mom's remembrance, there were no dramatic bagpipes or sentimental sing-a-longs. Pop would never stand to be fussed over, in life or in death. His only request was that some of his ashes be spread over the deep blue waters of Lake Powell, the site of many family gatherings, and where we had scattered the ashes of Bill and Mom. All Pop really wanted was to be with them again.

When I received my small vial of his ashes, I knew what I would do. Among family and friends, Pop was known for his apple pies, frequently baking up a few to give away. For the perfect pie, he insisted, you have to use the Northern Spy variety. On Father's Day, I carefully raked his atoms into the soil at the base of my own Northern Spy apple tree.

With all the sad formalities complete, I returned to my own mission, one that I had hoped to fulfill before my father passed away. As painful as it was to relive those deep conversations with Pop, I also found it to be a much-needed diversion, a way to cope with my grief. And so, every day after work,

I would spend some time transcribing Pop's words. Gradually, fragments turned into paragraphs, paragraphs into chapters. Still, I was not satisfied with the result. Frustrated, I realized that every one of Pop's detailed answers to my questions spawned yet more questions, endless gaps that I could never fill.

I wondered about the other sixteen missions my father had completed. Were they merely routine, or had they simply been overshadowed by the dangers of Schiphol and the catastrophe of number 18? I also wondered which of the crew members it was who had called to thank Pop for saving his life. And what would Pop think of this book if he were here to read it? So many questions.

And time was up.

✈ ✈
✈ ✈
✈ ✈

A year and a half later, my father's stories were still just a file on the computer. But for me, many things had changed. My job as a winemaker no longer fulfilled me; my best friend and business partner was leaving the state; the garage band in which I played guitar was evicted from our long-time mountaintop studio; the COVID-19 pandemic was still raging; and the pleasures of living in Sonoma County had literally gone up in flames. Worst of all, just one year after my father's memorial, my brother Jeff had passed away after battling brain cancer. In the space of a few years, I had lost both of my brothers, as well as my parents. It was more than a lot to take in. I needed a change, a change of my own making.

One day, I came home from work and told Lo that I wanted to leave California and move to New Mexico, and for some reason, she agreed. After twenty-five years, suddenly, on a whim, we were selling our house, downsizing and packing, knee-deep in complicated arrangements. I kept wondering what my father would say if he were here to render an opinion on this abrupt end to our California dream. Going through closets and mostly taking no prisoners, I once again came across the box of memorabilia that my grandmother had started collecting while Pop was at war. Inside, among the old papers and photographs, was the video of him reuniting with the last B-26. Lo had already packed the DVD player, so I turned to *YouTube*.

It seemed like years since I had watched the video. It reminded me that I still had not fulfilled my mission to tell my father's stories. I had been stumped and vexed by the gaps that could no longer be filled by talking to him. Now, in the middle of the chaos of preparing to move across the country, I once again felt motivated to tell Pop's story. Watching the video, I hoped to glean some new information, some important insight I may have missed.

Incredibly, the video had nearly a quarter million views as well as several hundred comments. I had been long overdue for a catharsis. After several viewings, I turned to the comments section. My tears flowed freely as I scrolled down the screen.

You guys are tremendous to do that for an old vet who gave so much for his country. He gave his todays for our tomorrows. Thumbs up. He can die a happy man!

Great story Mr. Wasowicz and a wonderful delivery of it! I saw it all happening in my mind as you described it, like reading a book. Thank you for your service Sir to the USA, in an endeavor that brought peace and freedom to hundreds of millions!

A story beautifully told. A piece of history so wonderfully recorded. Mr Wasowicz is an amazing gentleman—so sharp for his age—with the ability to share this 70 year old piece of history all of us. Thank you Mr Wasowicz for your service. Thank you for sharing your story. You are my hero.

Please whoever is cutting all these onions, stop, I can't even see the screen.

In my life, I have had the honor and privilege to meet many real, honest-to-God heroes. One thing that every one of them has had in common was that not one of them would acknowledge that he was a hero. Every one of them would tell you that he (or she) was just doing his job and the real hero was the guy next to him. Barney is exactly that kind of man. A true hero.

Thank you sir... that's all I can say... Thank you.

Men who didn't have a mean bone in their bodies, because of aggression of some countries, were asked to fire shots in anger. Those men and women gave the bloom of their youth to that cause. They have my undying respect and admiration. I would hope the Lord has a reserved spot for such great Americans when in the fullness of time, they are called home.

You say "They almost made me feel like I was a hero..." You are exactly that, Sir. A HERO in the truest sense of the word. Thank you.

As before, the outpouring of admiration and gratitude moved me deeply. It was beautiful. And yet, something about the well-meaning comments troubled me. I couldn't put it into words.

Then one day, ruminating while walking our dog Paco, I dimly recalled something that Pop had said. Returning to my notebooks, I flipped through the pages until I found it. There was one passage I had not transcribed, one that didn't seem to have a proper place. It was Pop's response to one of my many questions about that final mission, that unlucky mission number 18. Out of nowhere, he had lost his temper and interrupted me.

"You keep saying *YOU*," he had exclaimed, exasperated. I stared at him a few moments, wondering what he was talking about.

"Your questions. You keep asking, 'Where were *you* flying? How many bombs did *you* drop? How did *you* get out?'"

He paused, placing his hands over his eyes and pressing on the lids.

"It wasn't just me, Tony," he said wearily. "You have to realize that I was part of a *crew*. Part of a whole bomb squadron. We all worked together. We had each other's back. We were all in this together."

"I think I understand, Pop," I said aloud to the words in my notebook.

Eighty years ago, at the age of eighteen, my father set out to become a pilot. On his journey through World War II, he trained to fly B-26 Martin Marauders and became part of a cohesive crew. Together they trained, went to war, and completed seventeen missions serving for the United States Army Air Corps. On their eighteenth mission, their plane was shot down by a German fighter pilot, but they all survived. After being captured by German soldiers, the men were separated, interrogated, and taken to POW camps where they were starved and dehumanized until they were finally liberated by their Allies and sent home to their families.

That was it. That was the story from start to finish. Pop was never one to talk about himself, never one to tell war stories unless prompted. He had always insisted, "It was a case of *If you hadn't been there, done that, you wouldn't be able to really comprehend it.*"

And yet, I felt that I did grasp his meaning. Pop had defined himself not by his individual accomplishments and hardships, but by his sense of being part of something bigger than himself. Knowing everything about his experience in videographic detail would have been fascinating, but more important was recognizing the crucial theme of camaraderie, the one principle that properly summed up my father. And those of us who knew him, his family and friends and air mates, were lucky to have been part of his crew.

And yet.

There is still more. The truth is, I had always known these things about my father. All my life I saw how he was, steadfast and kind, quietly leading by example. For my whole life, he had been there. For the last two years of his life, I had asked for his life experience, and he had delivered. And now I would never be able to ask him anything again.

But in the end, it was not the answers that mattered. It was the asking.

Epilogue

Memory is the treasury and guardian of all things.

—Marcus Tullius Cicero

In Barth, Germany, a World War II prisoner-of-war camp called *Stalag Luft I* once held 9,000 men. One of those men was my father. Although the camp itself is long gone, the suffering that was endured there will be remembered.

Today, a quiet grassy field is all that remains of the barracks, barbed wire, and guard towers that robbed so many men of their liberty, comfort, and dignity. Three rows of trees symbolize the Allied Airmen imprisoned there and the Allies who liberated them: American Pine, British Oak, and Russian Birch. The trees form a triangle around a large granite boulder, a monument to the British and American former POWs. To one side, the flags of the United States, Great Britain, and Russia fly alongside the POW/MIA flag. On the boulder are two bronze plaques, one inscribed in German, the other in English:

This plaque is dedicated by the citizens of Barth and the Royal Air Force Ex-Prisoners of War Association on 28 September 1996 to commemorate all those held prisoner at Stalag Luft I, sited here from July 1940 to May 1945: members of the British Commonwealth and United States of American Air Forces and their Allies from the occupied countries and the Soviet Union.

"NOTHING HAS BEEN FORGOTTEN"

Pop's Apple Pie

7 large apples

Double pie crust

2 eggs

1 tbsp butter

¼ cup sugar

Nutmeg

Cinnamon

"Now pay close attention," Pop instructed. "The details are the most important part."

"I'm all ears. And eyes," I said. "And I'm writing all this down so I don't forget anything. Just don't mess it up because this will be passed down through generations."

I laughed. He didn't.

It starts with the apple. Pop always said that the very best apple for pie-making is the Northern Spy. He lamented the fact that it was impossible to find his favorite apple in the hot Southwest.

"You *can* use other apples," Pop conceded. "Delicious works well. I like Gala, too. But I do miss the days when we would take the station wagon out to the orchards, load up bushel baskets of Spys, and bake pies for everyone."

Today, the pie we were baking would be perfect. Three years earlier, I had purchased a bareroot Northern Spy tree from a farmer back East. This year, I had my first crop of twelve green-and-red-blushed apples. I picked them in the morning before my flight, and just hours later I stood over the kitchen sink, peeling the Northern Spys.

While I peeled the apples, Pop arranged all the ingredients on the counter. First, he cracked the two eggs, separating whites and yolks into two small bowls. Then he used a whisk to whip the whites till foamy.

"Preheat that oven to 425 degrees," he said. "You can make your own crust, or you can just buy one at the store. They're pretty good."

A package of Pillsbury pre-made piecrusts had been sitting out to soften up, and he now took one out of the package and spread it over the pie plate, tamping it down lightly with his fingers to cover the pan. He then used a small brush to coat the entire crust with egg whites. By then I had cut the apples into uniform slices.

"Now add the apples. But only half of them. Got that? Just add *half* of the sliced apples."

"Yes, sir!" I said.

"Now just give it a very light dusting of nutmeg. *Very* light. It's strong stuff and can overwhelm the flavor. And then the cinnamon. A little bit more than the nutmeg. Now add the rest of the apples."

When he was satisfied with the size and shape of the apple mound before him, he cut up the cold pat of butter and evenly distributed the tiny cubes over the apples.

"You want to spread the sugar on top last. And don't try and spread it perfectly even. That's important. Did you write that down? Just pour it randomly. There'll be some bare spots."

Next, he placed the top crust on the pie, pressing the dough along the edge of the pan. In one continuous motion he used a knife to trim the excess dough along the edge. Finally, he cut five small slots into the pie to let the steam escape, so that the apples wouldn't get too soft.

"Now dab some of the egg whites onto the top. And do it like the sugar, kind of in random patches. Don't do the edges, or they'll burn. Then just a tiny pinch of cinnamon to finish it off. *Tiny*."

He washed his hands, took off his apron and stood back, displaying his creation.

"It'll bake for about forty-five minutes, but that's just a guess. Knowing when to take it out, when it's finished, is the most important part of this. You can test it by poking the apples with a skewer, but I mostly use my nose. When it *smells* done, it *is* done.

He paused.

"And don't overcook it! Nobody likes mushy apple pie."

ACKNOWLEDGMENTS

Memory is an unreliable witness, but it's a start. This book is based on Tony's memories and conversations with Pop, who passed away before we could finish writing it. To fill the inevitable gaps, we drew on various sources, such as Internet research and documents preserved by Tony's family. We are not historians, but we have done our best to represent the context of Pop's stories accurately. We learned a lot.

Our many thanks go to John Stonecipher for flying Pop's crew to Florida; to Kermit Weeks, for opening his Air Museum to us; to Bryan Matuskey for filming Pop's reunion with the last B-26; to Mike Smith, founder of *Martin B-26 Marauder, B-26.com*, for sharing an invaluable resource; to Bob Esser for sharing his research into his grandfather, Pop's Radioman, Robert Carpenter; to our friend Linda Ross for reviewing the manuscript; and to Pop, of course, for everything.

BIBLIOGRAPHY

Allen, Trevor J. "WWII Martin B-26 Marauder Crews." *Martin B-26 Marauder*, Mike Smith, 2022, b26.com/historian/trevor_allen.htm.

"American Red Cross Prisoner of War Food Package No. 10." *National Museum of American History Behring Center*, Smithsonian, americanhistory.si.edu/collections/search/object/nmah_1092303.

"Amsterdam Airport Schiphol." *Wikipedia*, 17 Jan. 2023, en.wikipedia.org/wiki/Amsterdam_Airport_Schiphol.

"Camp Lucky Strike: RAMP Camp No. 1." *National World War II Museum New Orleans*, 26 June 2020, www.nationalww2museum.org/war/articles/camp-lucky-strike.

"Don't mention the War... but let's talk about the food." *The*, 28 Dec. 2020, www.thedefinitearticle.org/cuisine/dont-mention-the-war-but-lets-talk-about-the-food.

Dorr, Robert F. "Flying and Fighting in the B-26 Marauder The view from the cockpit." *Defense Media Network*, 1 Oct. 2012, www.defensemedianetwork.com/stories/flying-and-fighting-in-the-b-26-marauder/.

Drapeau, Roaul. "The Norden Bombsight: Was it Truly Accurate Beyond Belief?" *Warfare History Network*, Sovereign Media, 2023, warfarehistorynetwork.com/the-norden-bombsight-was-it-truly-accurate-beyond-belief/.

"Flak: myth versus reality with Donald Nijboer." *Hush-Kit: The alternative aviation magazine*, 25 Mar. 2021, hushkit.net/2021/03/25/flak-myth-versus-reality-with-donald-nijboer/.

"From muddy puddle to global hub." *Schiphol*, 2023, www.schiphol.nl/en/you-and-schiphol/page/airport-history/.

Gasior, Mariusz. "The Polish Pilots Who Flew In The Battle Of Britain." *Imperial War Museums*, 2022, www.iwm.org.uk/history/the-polish-pilots-who-flew-in-the-battle-of-britain.

"Greenland once truly green, scientists reveal." *CORDIS EU Research Results*, European Commission, 9 July 2007, cordis.europa.eu/article/id/28003-greenland-once-truly-green-scientists-reveal.

"History of Poland (1945-1989)." *New World Encyclopedia*, 27 Aug. 2022, www.newworldencyclopedia.org/entry/History_of_Poland_(1945-1989).

"Kermit Weeks." *Fantasy of Flight*, 2022, www.fantasyofflight.com/collection/.

Klier, Chester P. "Friday, July 30, 1943 - 386th Bomb Group Mission Number 1." *Martin B-26 Marauder*, Mike Smith, 2022, b26.com/historian/chester_klier/001.htm.

---. "In the Beginning, 386th Bomb Group." *Martin B-26 Marauder*, Mike Smith, 2022, b26.com/historian/chester_klier/in_the_beginning.htm.

---. "Monday, December 13, 1943 - 386th Bomb Group Mission Number 55." *Martin B-26 Marauder*, Mike Smith, 2022, www.b26.com/historian/chester_klier/055.htm.

"Manneken Pis." *Wonders of the World*, 2022, www.wonders-of-the-world.net/Manneken-Pis/.

"The Newspaper." *Stalag Luft I World War II - Prisoners of War - Stalag Luft I*, Mary Smith and Barbara Freer, daughters of Dick Williams, Jr, www.merkki.com/powwow.htm.

REUNITED - P.O.W. & The Last B-26. Directed by Bryan Matuskey, Guidance Aviation, 2015. *YouTube*, www.youtube.com/watch?v=Sr03I-djB1Qo.

Richard, Oscar G., III. "Hubert Zemke - A Man to Remember." *Stalag Luft I World War II - Prisoners of War - Stalag Luft I*, Mary Smith and Barbara Freer, daughters of Dick Williams, Jr, www.merkki.com/zemkehubert.htm.

"The Terrifying German 'Revenge Weapons' Of The Second World War." *Imperial War Museums*, 2023, www.iwm.org.uk/history/the-terrifying-german-revenge-weapons-of-the-second-world-war.

"Timeline." *Antwerp Commemorates World War II*, City of Antwerp, 2022, www.antwerpcommemorates.be/timeline.

Wilson, Stephen. "Rationing in World War II." *Historic UK.*, www.historic-uk.com/CultureUK/Rationing-in-World-War-Two/.

"World War II: D-Day, The Invasion of Normandy." *Dwight D. Eisenhower Presidential Library, Museum & Boyhood Home*, National Archives, www.eisenhowerlibrary.gov/research/online-documents/world-war-ii-d-day-invasion-normandy.

"World War II Radio Heroes: Letters of Compassion." Review of *World War II Radio Heroes: Letters of Compassion*, by Lisa Spahr and Austin Camacho. *Fandom*, 2022, military-history.fandom.com/wiki/World_War_II_Radio_Heroes:_Letters_of_Compassion.

Tony Wasowicz is the Volunteer Coordinator for the Santa Fe Animal Shelter. Lorraine is an Associate Instructor in the English department of Santa Rosa Junior College in California. Tony and Lorraine currently live in Santa Fe, New Mexico, following their dreams with their dog Paco.

✈ ✈
  ✈ ✈
✈ ✈

Made in the USA
Monee, IL
25 March 2023

29947041R10134